CW00407653

Published by KENTON PUBLISHING

The Granary, Hatham Green Lane, Stansted, SEVENOAKS, Kent TN15 7PL

+44 (0)1474 853 669

www.kentonpublishing.co.uk

Copyright © 2010 Paul Sneddon

The right of Paul Sneddon to be identified as the Author of the Work has been asserted by him in accordance with the Copyright, Designs and Patents Act 1988.

A CIP catalogue of this book is available from the British Library

First published in Great Britain in 2010 by KENTON PUBLISHING

ISBN 978-0-9546223-6-7

Typeset by Cannon Hill Services

Printed in the UK by Cromwell Press Group, Trowbridge, Wilts

Edited by Stuart Croll

Cover design by Damian Wilson

Cover photograph by Andy Barr

Illustrations by Paul Baker & Alex Collier

www.top50greatestscots.com

Every effort has been made to trace and contact copyright holders of all materials in this book. The author and publisher will be glad to rectify any omissions at the earliest opportunity.

All rights reserved. No part of this publication may be reproduced, stored in a retrieval system or transmitted, in any form or by any means, electronic, mechanical, photocopying, recording or otherwise, without the prior permission of the publisher.

Any copy of this book issued by the Publishers as casebound or as paperback is sold subject to the condition that it shall not, by way of trade or otherwise, be lent, resold, hired out or otherwise circulated without the Publisher's prior consent, in any form of binding or cover other than that in which it is published and without a similar condition including the condition being imposed on the subsequent purchaser

THE

TOP 50 GREATEST SCOTS OF ALL TIME... EVER!

To Annabel,

All the best,

x

By VLADIMIR McTAVISH

Art Direction by Damian Wilson

ACKNOWLEDGEMENTS

Edited by Stuart Croll

Additional Material by

Stuart Croll

Derek Johnston

Keir McAllister

Greg McHugh

John Scott

Kenny O'Brien

Michael Beck

Thanks for the invaluable assistance of

Kevin Anderson

Frankie Boyle

Jo Caulfield

Des Clarke

Julia Cloughley-Sneddon

Roseanne Cloughley-Sneddon

Jane McAllister

Fred Macaulay

The Stand Comedy Club

Artwork, Layout and Design

Damian Wilson

Additional Artwork

Patt Strickland

Thanks to Mike Ridley for having the idea in the first place and to my wife Christine for putting up with my stupidity

A wee word of support from Frankie Boyle

VLADIMIR MCTAVISH has been a friend of mine for many, many years.

He is not one of those comedians obsessed with his work. He will talk for hours about poetry, naval history or ceramics despite knowing nothing about those subjects. He has studied for years to become a Master of rai-ki jung, the ancient Japanese art of entering a room just as somebody is finishing a story and ruining it.

When Vladimir first told me he was writing a book I didn't hear him . When he later told me he was halfway through writing a book I was surprised. As I understand it, the original title for this book was Missed Fucking Opportunities and it was to be a Bukowskian re-telling of every sexual regret in Vlad's life.

I never read it, but I think this version is much better, a fine piece of work about a much more depressingly grim topic, Scotland and the Scots. For those who think of our nation simply as 'Ground Zero for SuperAids', this is the book for you.

Enjoy

Frankie Boyle

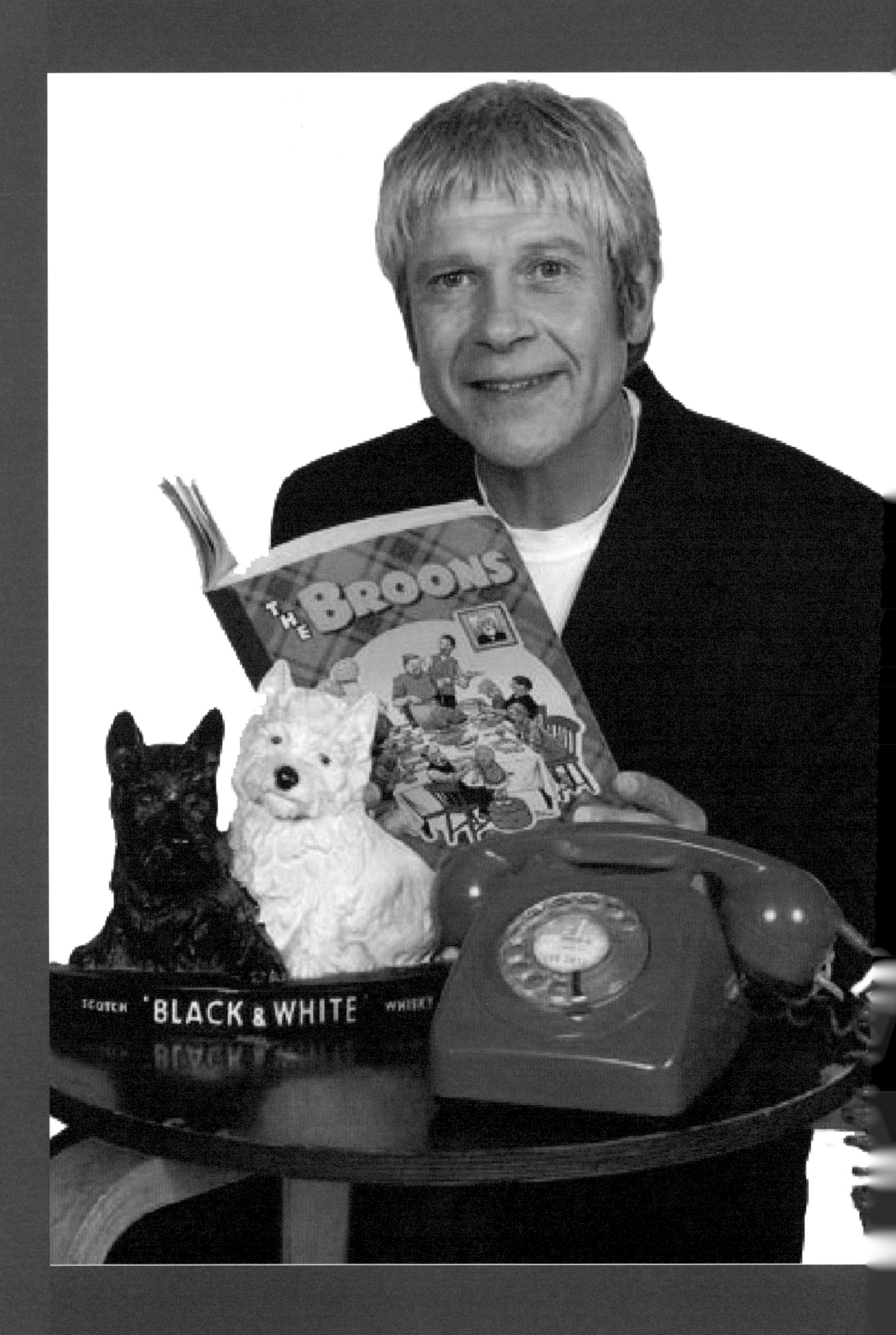
THE BROONS
SCOTCH 'BLACK & WHITE'

An introduction from Vladimir McTavish

THIS IS A BOOK ABOUT SCOTLAND AND THE Scottish people.

A nation of contradictions.

A proud nation, whose citizens have achieved much and contributed a great deal to global civilisation, yet a nation that is often embarrassed by itself and its own culture

We are justly proud of inventing the television yet who doesn't cringe when they watch Postcode Challenge.

This translates into how we are viewed abroad.

In the late 1700s, the radical French philosopher Voltaire declared: "It is to Scotland that we look for our ideas of civilisation."

However, in 2003 the Lonely Planet Guide described Scotland as: "A land full of anti-English sentiment poisoned by binge-drinking and sectarian bigotry."

The truth, as ever, lies somewhere in between.

This is a book of lists.

We live in a list-obsessed age.

I personally have reached the time in life when I am drawn to magazine articles suggesting "One Hundred Things To Do Before You Die".

They then proceed to suggest kayaking across Hudson Bay, paragliding over the Grand Canyon and skiing down Mount Kilimanjaro.

Personally I cannot help thinking on reading such lists: "Bloody Hell, I could actually die doing half of the things I have to do before I die!"

Until recently, The Scotsman newspaper used to publish a pull-out list section every Wednesday, 'The Scotsman Recommends'. Each week they suggested the best places to find scones in Pitlochry or the best beaches in Scotland.

Which is all well and good.

But it does not give the full panorama of the Scottish experience.

They never had, for example:

The Five Best Towns in Scotland to Buy Heroin.

Top Five Bus Stations to Get Noised-Up by Neds Drinking Alcopops.

Scotland's Top Five beaches To Find a Corpse.

In this book, I am seeking to redress that cultural balance

This book celebrates Scotland's successes and its failures.

It could just as well have been titled Heroes, Villains and Numpties.

The people who appear in this book are, like Scotland itself, a mixture of the good, the bad and the ludicrous.

Some of them are Truly Good. Some of them are Truly Evil. Most of them are Completely Ridiculous.

You will almost certainly not agree with the order and there will possibly be a favourite eminent Scot not included in my list - but, hey, we love an argument don't we?

This book glories in our boorishness as much as it does in our sophistication.

For the simple reason that that's what we are like.

"Here's tae us, wha's like us? Fair few, an' aw deid!"

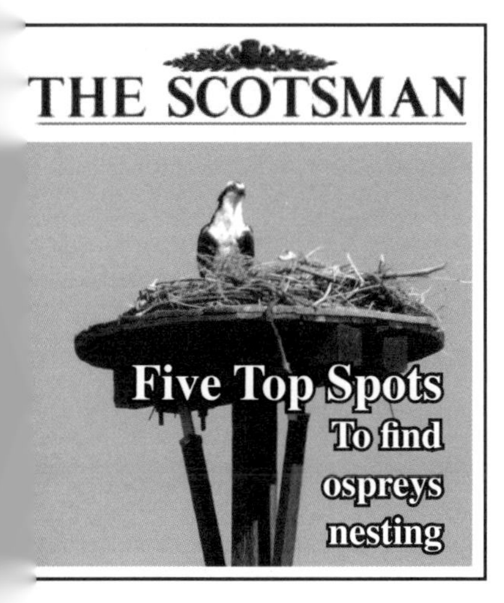

SO WHO ARE OUR TOP 50 AND WHY?

I have chosen 50 Scots who embody the essential nature of our nation.

Their exploits cover the full gamut of human endeavour: Science, Sport, Entertainment, The Arts, Music, Politics, Religion, Drinking, Enterprise, Crime and Cruelty.

Quite a few Scots managed to multi-task and to find fame or notoriety in a variety of fields.

The following should suggest this is a bad idea:

JIMMY BOYLE
Successfully managed to follow up a career in crime with a career in the arts. Anyone who has seen any of his sculptures will agree he was pretty brutal at both.

ANDY GORAM
Uniquely in the modern age, found fame in two sports: cricket and football. Found more notoriety due to his associations with religion, drinking and sex.

DONALD FINDLAY
Greatly respected for his knowledge of criminal law. Less well-respected for famously mixing, alcohol, religion and music (but never sex) at a sporting function.

50 Elvis Presley

A CONTROVERSIAL CHOICE TO START our list of the 50 Greatest Scots of All Time Ever. At first glance, Elvis Presley, the king of rock and roll, may not be regarded as Scottish but his roots have been traced back to Aberdeenshire.

And if there was ever any need to provide compelling evidence that Elvis was one of Jock Tamson's bairns, he died of a heart attack at the age of 42 – what could be more Scottish than that?

We are a sick nation. How sick? We gave the world the bagpipes. That's pretty sick.

The daily papers are for ever full of stories predicting doom and gloom on the health front.

Recently a headline in The Scotsman warned us:

SCOTLAND SITTING ON A DIABETES AND HEART DISEASE TIMEBOMB

Imagine if one of them went off. What a mess that would make.

Despite, or perhaps because of, being an unhealthy people we have given much to the advancement of medical science...

Alexander Fleming 49

AYRSHIRE-BORN ALEXANDER FLEMING'S discovery of penicillin is estimated to have saved more than 200 million lives.

And the wonderful feature of Fleming's breakthrough was that it was a fluke.

Working at St Mary's Hospital in Paddington, London he had developed a reputation as a brilliant researcher but also a lazy and untidy lab technician.

While on holiday he had left a clutter of plates growing various bacteria just lying around on his desk.

When he returned he threw the dishes into disinfectant.

He soon noticed an area on the dishes where the bacteria could not grow.

From further investigations he had discovered penicillin – the first bacteria killer or antibiotic. And, to this day, the first medication offered to sufferers of syphilis.

A by-product of both his scientific genius and chronic untidiness.

I shared a student flat in the 1970s with a guy from Aberdeen who, unless I'm very much mistaken, invented penicillin all over again. Completely by accident.

However, it didn't appear to help his syphilis.

In 1945 Fleming was awarded the Nobel Prize for medicine proving an inspiration to scientists and untidy people everywhere.

And although he died in 1955 the awards just keep coming in Fleming's direction.

In 2009, he became the face of the Clydesdale Bank's five pound note and as this is the one Scottish bank not owned by the taxpayer he can look out at us without embarrassment.

Fleming and his appearance on a bank note encapsulate the entire spectrum of Scots living in London. Namely, that 33% are doctors, 33% are bankers and 33% are sufferers of syphilis.

48 Chris Hoy

BEFORE THE BEIJING OLYMPICS NOBODY APART from the most fervent cycling fan had heard of Chris Hoy.

In other words, ten people had heard of Chris Hoy.

Everyone in Scotland was amazed when he won three gold medals for cycling. Some people were amazed that there were three different types of cycling. Most people were amazed that cycling was a sport.

Until then, cycling was a quick way of getting to the pub without getting breathalysed. And on the way home you usually fell off the bike. (Well, at any rate, that's what normally happened on Dumbarton Road in Partick on a Saturday night).

However following his three gold medals, Hoy became a household name, a national treasure and even had a cool nickname – The Real McHoy.

Chris actually was inspired to take up cycling as a child in the 1980s after seeing the movie ET. And no one would be surprised now were he to get a bike to fly.

Hoy is an incredible physical specimen. The training regime required of a top cyclist means he has developed thighs twice the width of the average man.

Hoy had become Scotland's most successful Olympian winning more golds than legends such as Eric Liddell, Alan Wells and David Wilkie.

He even won the BBC Sports Personality of the Year award.

Hoy was too good.

Where was the Scottish trait of glorious failure?

Just when everyone thought Hoy might not be Scottish he managed to assure us all that he was definitely a true-born Scot.

In his first competitive race since Olympic glory he fell off his bike and with that crash he proved he was human. Not unlike the average jakey on Dumbarton Road on a Saturday night.

And we loved him all the more because of it!

Sherlock Holmes 47

THE BIRTHPLACE OF SHERLOCK HOLMES is the subject of much conjecture amongst fans of the great detective.

The major reason for this debate is of course that Sherlock Holmes was a fictional character.

But without Scotland there would have been no Sherlock Holmes.

He was the creation of Edinburgh-born doctor Arthur Conan Doyle, who wrote four novels and 56 short stories featuring Sherlock Holmes.

And through astute observation and deductive reasoning the detective solved the trickiest of cases.

Conan Doyle, when asked if there was a real Sherlock Holmes, always maintained that Holmes was inspired by Dr Joseph Bell, for whom Doyle had worked as a clerk at the Edinburgh Royal Infirmary.

Like Sherlock Holmes, Bell was noted for drawing large conclusions from the smallest observations.

And Holmes had another Scottish trait in that he was a drug user.

On the positive side Sherlock Holmes has created work for thousands of actors, directors and producers.

Sherlock Holmes is the fictional character most adapted to the performing arts.

The adventures of Sherlock Holmes have been transformed for theatre, ballet, film, radio and television.

Sadly, in all those sixty stories Sherlock Holmes never had to solve any mysteries in Scotland until in a dusty old second hand bookshop, I discovered this short story:

SHERLOCK HOLMES AND THE CASE OF THE MUTANT MONKEY MURDERER!

Turn over for more....

Sherlock Holmes the mutant

DOCTOR WATSON AND I HAD SPENT AN enjoyable fortnight in Edinburgh, a most handsome city I may add, and one which appears to be devoid of Scots. At any rate, devoid of those Scots of the lower orders who appear to speak in a foreign tongue.

Indeed, at the small lodging house in which we were accommodated in the city's most splendid "New Town", our neighbours were as genteel as one would expect to find in Kensington or Knightsbridge.

And our landlady, Miss Jeannie Stevenson, was most accommodating and would keep her doors open to guests no matter what the hour of night.

Watson had had to travel North to attend to the affairs of his aunt. A lady, it must be said, greatly prone to affairs. For myself, it allowed me the opportunity to visit the city of my birth and to re-acquaint myself with an old colleague, Inspector Finlay McLaverty, once of Scotland Yard but now of the City of Edinburgh Constabulary. Indeed, it had been on his recommendation that we had booked into Miss Stevenson's lodgings, a beautiful town house decorated in the Turkish style, where we appeared to be the only guests staying for longer than a single night. Indeed, some guests seemed to stay no longer than an hour or so.

"They're only after a knee-trembler, Mr Holmes," Miss Stevenson had explained, no doubt in reference to some quaint local custom. Despite the brevity of these visits, Miss Stevenson employed all manner of different chambermaids. They appeared to come from all corners of the globe - Scandinavia, France and China.

"I cater for all tastes, Mr Holmes," Miss Stevenson had said enigmatically, as she winked in a manner I have not seen before. On his return, Watson and I had spent a most enjoyable afternoon perambulating the splendid zoological gardens and were just sitting down to afternoon tea with our affable hostess, who seemed to offer all range of fare.

"I also do French or Greek, Mr Holmes. If that's what takes your fancy," she offered. I was on the point of saying that English afternoon tea would suffice when there came a knock at the door. "Ooh, who can want to grab my knockers at this time of day?" exclaimed our landlady.

I HEARD THE MAID ANSWER AND A VOICE outside exclaim: "An urgent telegram for a Mr Sherlock Holmes." The telegram in question was from my old acquaintance, Inspector McLaverty, and it described a crime of the most gruesome nature.

"Watson," I uttered, although the colour had left my cheeks, "We must make for the Grassmarket where a most ghastly murder has been committed."

"Ignore it, Holmes, probably just another prostitute," suggested Watson, a remark that drew a most distasteful retort from Miss Stevenson which should not be repeated in polite company.

"No, Watson," I explained. "It is a normal upstanding member of the public. A street hot-food vendor has been brutally killed and abused in the most obscene manner with his own stock-in-trade."

Watson's visage took on the pallor of a ghost as he too read from McLaverty's message. "Good God, Holmes. What kind of monster is at large?"

"That is for us to find out, Watson. Let us hail a cab and make the utmost haste to the Grassmarket! We have no time for tea, I fear, Miss Stevenson."

"Not even for a wee bit of crumpet? You look the kind of man who likes a little nibble on something. The offer's still open when you get back."

"On our return, Miss Stevenson, Watson and I will enter through the back passage..." I shouted, as I climbed into the cab.

"Aye, we cater for that too, Mr Holmes."

"In cases like these, it is important to protect our anonymity, you understand."

"Don't worry, gentlemen, your secret's safe with me." An again she gave that wink whose significance at the time escaped me.

ON ARRIVAL AT THE GRASSMARKET, WE were confronted by a most gruesome scene. The hot-food vendor lay under his cart, dead as a doornail but with a look of utter horror forever etched on his face.

"Poor man didnae have a chance," explained McLaverty. "Been hit about the head with a blunt instrument. And then raped with one of his own sausages!"

"Good Lord!" exclaimed Watson.

"A hot one... straight out of the boiler. Must have burned on the way up!" continued McLaverty.

"My God, Holmes, we're dealing with a psychopath!"

"Perhaps we are, Watson. And then, perhaps we are not. Let us examine the crime scene, and make judgements based on facts and not emotions. I would surmise, from my initial assessment, that the murderer may well have been a vegetarian."

"Good gracious, Holmes, what makes you think that?" uttered Watson.

"Aye?" echoed McLaverty.

"Examine the evidence. Most murderers, whatever their motive, would either have eaten the sausage or stolen it an sold it for cash. Our murderer, on the other hand, chooses to brutally insert a hot sausage into the anus of his victim. Hardly the work of a meat-eater, I would suggest."

"My goodness, Holmes, that's astounding," uttered Wats

"Aye!" echoed McLaverty.

"Inspector, McLaverty. Please compile a list of all known vegetarians in the city. We must interview them all with gre haste..."

It was then that I was interrupted by a bestial grunting a a blood-curdling scream from an adjacent street, followed

and the case of monkey murderer

he familiar sound of a police whistle and cries of "Murder! Murder! He's struck again!"

McLaverty, Watson and I followed these cries around he corner where we were met with a picture of the most nhumane brutality. A uniformed policeman stood by the ody.

"He's struck again, Sir," he struggled to utter the words. This time it's a newspaper seller. When I found him, he'd ad the property section stuffed up his arse and set on fire."

"Don't jump to conclusions, Campbell," warned McLaverty. You never know, that wound could have been self-inflicted."

"I doubt it, Sir. These chaps are on commission. Plus it was vedged so far up, there was smoke coming out of his ears. Vhat kind of killer are we dealing with, Sir?"

"Clearly a maniac," opined Watson.

"Aye," echoed McLaverty.

MY RESPONSE TOOK THEM BOTH BY surprise. "A maniac, no doubt. But clearly also a member of the higher social order, almost certainly an ex-public schoolboy."

"However did you reach that conclusion, Holmes?" I could ead the incredulity in Watson's voice.

"Aye?" echoed McLaverty.

"A member of the working classes or lower social order ould not have burned this copy of the Edinburgh Evening ews intact, as indeed intact it is," I explained. "As they ould have been tempted to keep page twenty-three. 'Why ge twenty-three?' you may ask."

"Indeed, Holmes, why page twenty-three?" responded a mused Watson.

"Aye?" echoed McLaverty.

"Because, unless I am very much mistaken, it is on page enty-three this day, and every Thursday that the Spot-e-Ball coupon is printed. Our killer clearly has no need of e three shillings and sixpence in prizemoney."

"That's astounding, Holmes!"

"Aye," echoed McLaverty.

"Believe you me, McLaverty, when you've been in this me as long as I have you develop a sixth sense."

And with this I turned to leave, only to collide with an eedingly large woman who was running towards me with ror in her eyes. We both fell to the ground. Picking myself I shouted, "Can you not look where you're going, for d's sake?"

o which her only answer was, "Help! Polis! Murder!"

Don't exaggerate, woman," I shouted in reply. "Someone well-padded as you are can take a fall to the ground hout injury!"

No, sir, no' you. Yon murdering beast, he's struck again. ther yin's deid, och aye we're aw' doomed!"

Whatever is this woman going on about, McLaverty? you translate?"

t looks like he's struck again, Mr Holmes."

An assertation seemingly confirmed by the woman herself. "Aye, ya glaikit fucker," she wailed in her bizarre argot. "I'm jist eftir telling ye, the cunting murderer's struck again!"

"Screw the nut, ya daft bint!" shouted McLaverty. "We don't want to cause a panic."

But the woman was not listening. And her blood-churning story carried on thus, "I seen him. He was up there on the roof of the catherdral...he looked like he was half-man, half-monkey.

"Then someone got a bird shite on their face, and the monkey thing jumped on them and dragged them doon a dark alley. I was that close a bit of the bird shite hit me on the airm." And she pointed to a stain on her sleeve. Which was where Watson's medical training was invaluable.

"Bird droppings?" he queried as he rubbed her arm. "Unless I'm mistaken," he opined, on tasting the deposit. "That's human ejaculate."

"Are you certain of that, Watson?"

"Never surer, Holmes, I'd recognise the taste anywhere. Don't forget I spent six years as a naval surgeon."

"You know what this means, Watson? He's marking out his victims!"

"Aye," echoed McLaverty.

"Noo you mention it," the woman volunteered, "he did look like he was rubbing his cock. But I thought nothing of it."

"Yes," I replied, "You probably see that kind of thing all the time, don't you, madam?"

"But, Holmes," interjected Watson, "what kind of a monster are we dealing with here?"

"Aye?" echoed McLaverty.

"Like I say," explained the woman, "he was half-man, half-monkey."

THIS CLEARLY TAXED MCLAVERTY'S patience. "Yes, yes, we've heard the 'half-man-half-monkey' bit already, madam. Say it again and that could be construed as wasting police time. Now move along, don't want to get in the way of our enquiries. Especially not someone as fat as you are, madam."

"Haud on you, I've got a thyroid problem!"

"Madam," countererd MvLaverty, "the problem is your thyroid's exceedingly big..."

"I've been on a diet. I've given up pies. I don't eat sausages."

'Madam, would you care to repeat what you just said," I requested.

"I said, 'I don't eat sausages'."

"Inspector McLaverty! Arrest this woman at once on suspicion of murder. We've found our maniac."

"Trying to confuse us with her stories of half-men half-monkeys," scoffed Watson.

"Aye!" echoed McLaverty.

TO BE CONTINUED... (Turn to Page 68)

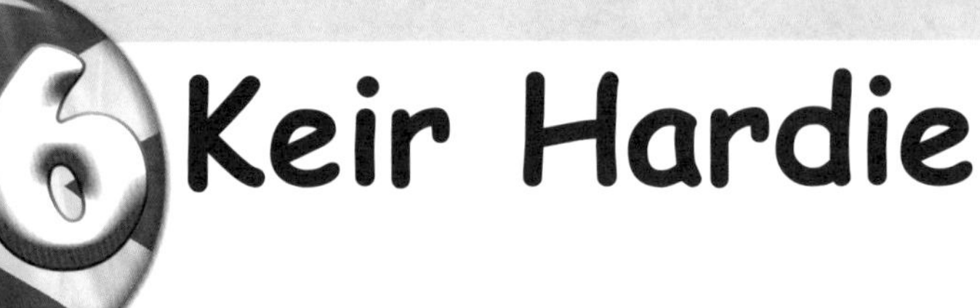

46 Keir Hardie

Parliamentary Election,
1906.
Borough of Merthyr Tydfil.
Address to the Electors
BY
J. Keir Hardie
THE
LABOUR CANDIDATE

FOR A SMALL NATION, SCOTLAND HAS historically punched above its weight in the field of politics.

Perhaps it's our belief in justice and democracy, perhaps it's our interest in economics and perhaps it's our love of an argument.

Scots have made a contribution to all the main political parties but it is in the Labour movement, in particular, that the most profound impact has been made.

And none more so than Keir Hardie.

He was the first Independent Labour Party member to be voted into Parliament - seven years before the founding of the Labour Party itself.

And it was he who organised a meeting of various trade unions and socialist groups and they agreed to form a Labour Representation Committee, and from that the Labour Party was born.

At the beginning of the last century the west coast of Scotland was a hotbed for radical politics.

The nearest the UK has ever come to a working-class revolution took place in Glasgow in 1919.

What started as a rent strike, turned into a full-scale uprising in George Square.

British tanks and troops were sent onto the streets of the city and shots were fired at the mob. There were many casualties and even more arrests.

Central to the revolt, which became known as Red Clydeside, were three men: EMMANUEL SHINWELL (later to became a Labour MP and cabinet minister and eventually a Life Peer), JAMES MAXTON (elected as an Independent Labour MP in the 1945 General Election) and the immortal JOHN MACLEAN

While history has given MacLean most of the credit, this may be due in no small part to the fact that at the time he took almost all the blame.

Jailed for sedition and ostracised later by his former comrades, he died a broken man.

Yet it took fully sixty years for another political activist to unite the Scottish people and re-ignite that spirit of revolutionary zeal and that person was...

...MARGARET THATCHER!

No-one has united the Scots in the same way that Thatcher did.

The entire country hated her.

Even the Scottish Tories hated her.

And she hated the Scots.

Thatcher alone must take all the credit for devolution.

Nobody was that bothered about independence until she came along.

When Thatcher was in power, hating the English was not a sentiment mired in small-mindedness, xenophobia or racism - it was a political statement.

In fact, when Thatcher was in power even the English hated the English.

But to return to KEIR HARDIE. To this day he is still revered inside the Labour Party and is highly respected outside it.

For a political leader of significance, Hardie has the distinction of having rarely been attacked in print after his death. This is largely down to the integrity of the man himself.

He built the Labour Party on a solid foundation of socialist principles. A legacy very much ignored by Gordon Brown.

Gordon Brown

GORDON BROWN IS A DEEPLY TRAGIC character, almost Shakespearean in nature. In fact, Brown's career reads very much like the plot of Macbeth but the Bard's story is dramatically more interesting towards the end.

The similarities are there for all to see.

For years, it is predicted that Macbeth will become the leader of the nation.

He schemes, connives and bullies his way to the top, stabbing friend and foe alike in the back on his way up.

And when he reaches that ultimate position of power, it all ends in horrific, dramatic bloodbath.

Likewise with Gordon Brown.

For years, it is predicted that he would become the leader of the nation.

He schemes, connives and bullies his way to the top, stabbing friend and foe alike in the back on his way up. And when he reaches that ultimate position of power, it turns out that he's a bit shit at the job.

Having turned his back on socialism, he has now made a complete mess of trying to run a capitalist economy.

So those of us who doubted his left-wing credentials may have been wrong all along. He could have been involved in a ten-year-long plot to bring down capitalism by undermining the system from within. On reflection, it's more likely he's just a bit shit at the job.

Brown is very unpopular in England.

People don't trust him – mainly because he's Scottish

What a lot of people down South fail to realise is that he is equally unpopular in Scotland.

We don't trust him either – mainly, because he pretends not to be Scottish.

He made himself particularly unpopular in Scotland immediately after becoming Prime Minister when he announced that the government were going to spend three million pounds of taxpayers' money on a state funeral for Margaret Thatcher.

My reaction to that news was: "Brilliant idea! Why wait till she dies?"

Brown is always banging on about Britishness, a concept that is fairly alien to 90% of the population of the UK and to about 99% of the population of Scotland.

Brown wants every immigrant who comes to the UK to sit a test to prove how "British" they are.

I took the test and failed it - albeit deliberately. Hence, I have devised a test of my own. It is a measure of "Scottishness"...

The semi-officia

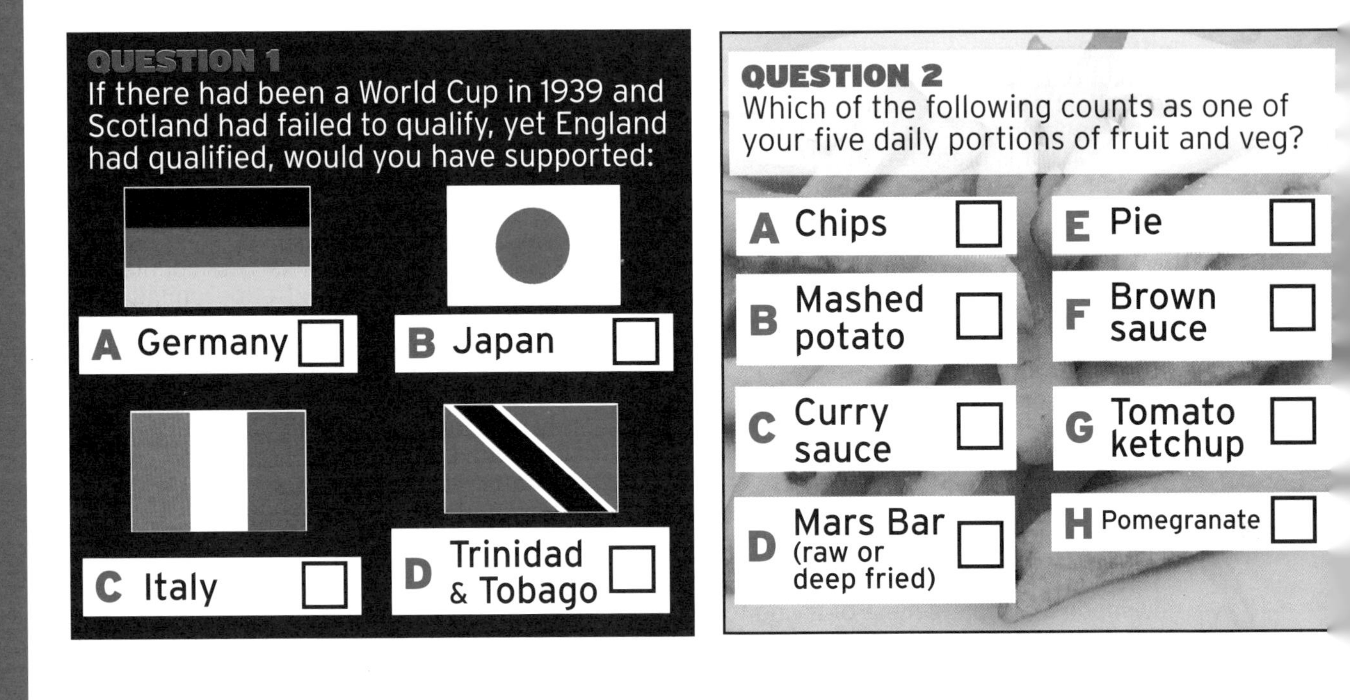

QUESTION 1
If there had been a World Cup in 1939 and Scotland had failed to qualify, yet England had qualified, would you have supported:

- A Germany ☐
- B Japan ☐
- C Italy ☐
- D Trinidad & Tobago ☐

QUESTION 2
Which of the following counts as one of your five daily portions of fruit and veg?

- A Chips ☐
- B Mashed potato ☐
- C Curry sauce ☐
- D Mars Bar (raw or deep fried) ☐
- E Pie ☐
- F Brown sauce ☐
- G Tomato ketchup ☐
- H Pomegranate ☐

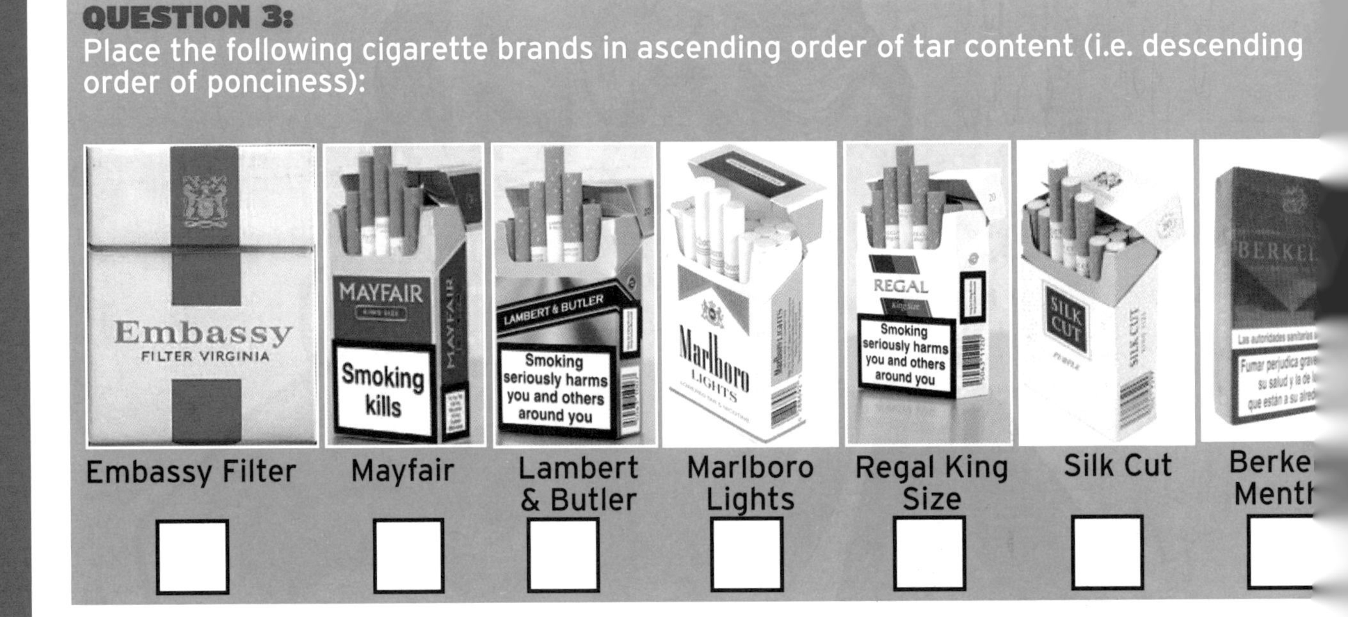

QUESTION 3:
Place the following cigarette brands in ascending order of tar content (i.e. descending order of ponciness):

Embassy Filter ☐ | Mayfair ☐ | Lambert & Butler ☐ | Marlboro Lights ☐ | Regal King Size ☐ | Silk Cut ☐ | Berke Ment ☐

Scottishness test

QUESTION 4
A four-letter swear word beginning with "C" is commonly used in the Scots vernacular. Its original meaning is:

- [ ] A part of the female anatomy
- [ ] An insult
- [ ] Term of endearment applied to your best friend on a night out on the bevvy
- [ ] Jeremy Kyle
- [ ] All of the above.

QUESTION 5
Which of the following phrases best sums up your attitude to life?

- [ ] The glass is half full
- [ ] The glass is half empty
- [ ] My ancestors once had a glass but it was stolen by the English
- [ ] Who needs a glass? You can tank it straight out of the bottle!
- [ ] Glass? I'll glass you, ya cunt!

We're doomed,
I say...doomed!

A NUMBER OF POLITICIANS' SPEECHES ARE written by people working in show business such as comedy writers.

If one Scottish comedy character was around today he would be writing Gordon Brown's speeches, and he'd be number 44 on my list.

Private Fraser from the long-running BBC sitcom Dad's Army was one of the most famous fictional Scots ever written.

And John Laurie - the Shakespearean actor who played Fraser - is credited with creating the notorious "We're doomed" catchphrase after the writers - Croft and Perry - overheard him complaining about an aspect of the show Laurie thought was doomed to failure.

Is Private Fraser the most famous fictional Scottish character?

Perhaps the most famous fictional character is the Loch Ness monster. However, the myth that was built up around Nessie in the 19th century was merely an example of some early, yet sophisticated, marketing by th local tourist industry. This led to a trend in personality tourist advertising.

Both Ayrshire and Dumfries trade on their Robert Burns connections.

Visitors to Edinburgh can follow the Robert Louis Stevenson trail, or go on a Rebus Tour.

For some reason known only to the Ci Fathers, Dundee has not been re-brande as "Dennis the Menace Country".

Even Ecclefechan attempts to attract visitors with a brown sign on the M74 advertising it as the birthplace of Thom Carlyle. OK, Thomas Carlyle might not bring in more than a handful of tourists a year.

But it's a handful more than would ever think of visiting

Private Fraser

Ecclefechan otherwise. However, it is the birthplace of a fictional character that has been at issue in a bitter geographical dispute in search of the tourist dollar.

Several Scottish towns have campaigned to be officially known as the official birthplace of SCOTTY FROM STAR TREK.

Chief engineer of the Starship SS Enterprise, Scotty was regarded as a miracle worker for solving any engineering problems the spaceship encountered. While the year of his birth is genuinely agreed to be 2222, his birthplace is a matter of much heated debate.

Most vocal of the claimants is Linlithgow in West Lothian.

Apparently in a novel – *Vulcan's Glory* – it is mentioned that Scotty was born there. But among Star Trek historians (yes, such people do exist!) the novels are not considered "fact."

A number of Trekkies claim that Scotty's hails from Aberdeen as in one early episode he described himself as "an old Aberdeen pub crawler."

Which sounds like it could be a euphemism, on a par with "I need more thrust, captain".

However, had Scotty actually existed, he would surely have been born in Cumbernauld, pictured here.

Or perhaps that's where Spock comes from.

Were this argument not ridiculous enough, the actor who played Scotty – James Doohan (left) – was so inept at doing a Scottish accent that most viewers thought he was Irish!

Doohan was doubtless aware of the argument over his character's birthplace and did not want a similar controversy to surround the whereabouts of Scotty's last resting place.

So, in his will, he laid down instructions for his ashes to be blasted into outer space in a rocket.

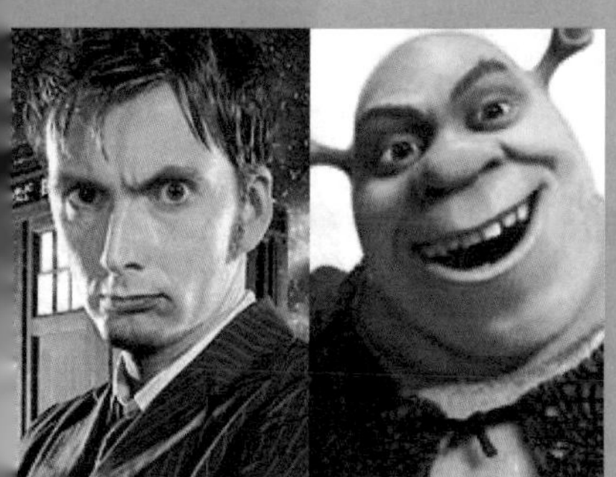

IN THE WORLD OF MOVIES THE SCOTTISH accent has come to the fore with thanks to Canadian Mike Myers. Myers was the vocal talent behind Shrek – a reclusive and grumpy ogre who lives in a swamp.

It is instructive to see how Scots are portrayed in fiction, when the creators of that fiction are themselves Scottish, compared to how they are painted when the writers of that fiction are English or American.

For example: MISS JEAN BRODIE (invented by a Scot) Intellectual, yet sexually alluring. Encouraging, enigmatic but with slightly suggestive Nazi sympathies versus MRS DOUBTFIRE (an American invention) Fat, domineering, incompetent, can be played on-screen by a man.

Dr Who (portrayed on TV by a Scot, DAVID TENNANT): Witty, sophisticated, handsome, phlegmatic versus SHREK (re-voiced on screen by a Scots-Canadian), an oversized green social misfit.

REBUS (invented by a Scot living in Scotland and played by Scot Ken Stott): Rogue genius, maverick, alcoholic versus SHERLOCK HOLMES (invented by a Scot living in England): Rogue genius, maverick, drug addict. And who do you think the most recognised Scot is throughout the World? Sean Connery? Billy Connolly? Gordon Brown? Lulu? Gail Porter? No, it's another fictional character. According to a worldwide poll carried out by The Times in 2005, the most recognisable Scot in the world is GROUNDSKEEPER WILLIE from The Simpsons.

©Matt Groening

Umpire, ya blind Masonic prick! That was a goal! That ball was right in the fucking net!
84 mph

Andy Murray 43

ANDREW MURRAY HAS THE POTENTIAL TO become one of Scotland's sporting greats.

Ranked as the fourth-best tennis player in the world by the age of 21. Indeed, the greatest measure of his success is that the BBC now considers him to be "British".

This success came after he was forced to sit out Wimbledon in 2007, due to a wrist injury.

He was twenty years old at the time.

You wonder how he managed to "injure his wrist".

Despite all this success, he has yet to totally win round the Scottish sporting public.

I would love to see the Tartan Army descending on Wimbledon, with sales of Buckfast and pies outstripping those of strawberries and champagne.

And can you imagine what might happen were he actually to win the Men's Singles at Wimbledon?

As if all this on-court success were not enough, by the age of 21, young Andy had already brought out his autobiography.

I don't know if anyone's read it.

I don't know if he's read it, I'm pretty certain he didn't write it.

Must have been an interesting meeting at the publishers

"What am I going to write about? All I've done is stayed at my mum's and played tennis"

"Write about your life, Andrew"

"But that's all I've done. Apart from the wrist injury, and I don't want to write about that..."

How the fuck's he got 15? He's only hit the ball once!

ANDY MURRAY COULD BECOME A SPORTING LEGEND of the future but this man is very much a sporting legend of the past.

Jim Baxter was one of the most skillful and cockiest footballers ever to play the beautiful game.

Baxter's indifference to discipline extended into every area of his life, ensuring that his career on the field was short and his time off it colourful.

He was a womaniser, a gambler and could drink Bacardi like he played football – intuitively and without a second thought.

The Fifer's alcoholism forced him to undergo two liver transplants later in life.

And yet these flaws make the legend greater still.

He even fires the imagination of Scots who weren't born when he played.

The bigger the occasion, the more Baxter relished it.

In seven domestic cup finals with Rangers he never lost, while two of his finest performances were for Scotland against England at Wembley.

In 1963, Slim Jim grabbed the right kind of double when ten-man Scotland beat the auld enemy in a 2-1 win.

Four years later Baxter surpassed that performance.

England were still undefeated after winning the World Cup ten months before but Scotland defeated Alf Ramsey's team 3-2 and became the unofficial world champions.

But the most endearing image from that game isn't a goal it is the grainy black and white clip of Baxter performing keepie-uppie with the ball by the touchline.

Baxter was not alone in being a Scottish footballer with a fondness for the bevvy. North of the Border, footie and booze have gone pretty much hand-in-hand down the year and the history of the beautiful game has been peppered with some less beautiful moments.

JIMMY JOHNSTONE's maritime exploits in Largs in 1974 have long left the realms of history and have now entered the realms of myth.

The wee winger went on a bender with a group of Scotland team mate and then decided to take to sea in a rowing boat with no oars. At 4 am, the coastguard had to be summone to rescue Jinky.

Yet amazingly, he wasn't droppe from the team.

Jim Baxter 42

In fact, not only did he start against England the ollowing Saturday, but he played a blinder, laying on both of Scotland's goals.

Less fortunate were the Copenhagen Five; Billy Bremner, Willie Young, Joe Harper, Arthur Graham and Pat McCluskey.

After defeating Denmark away from home, they were nvolved in a drinking session in a Copenhagen nightclub hat got so out of hand police in riot gear were called out. he five were banned for life.

And, of course, as well as being an on-pitch fiasco, let s not forget the multifarious off-pitch shenanigans in rgentina in 1978.

Perhaps cashing-in on the current fad for Seventies ostalgia, in 2009 Scotland players Barry Ferguson and llan McGregor were dropped from the team after an all-ight drinking session.

Yet, while Slim Jim Baxter and Jinky Johnstone would lence their critics through acts of genius on the park, e best the "Boozegate" pair could managed was an mbarrassingly crass act of juvenile petulance.

The pair of them are not fit to lace Jim Baxter's boots. owever, it must be said that Jim Baxter was quite often ot fit to lace Jim Baxter's boots.

41 Lisbon Lions

THE LIONS LINE-UP: Back row, from left – Jim Craig, Tommy Gemmell, Ronnie Simpson, Billy McNeill, Bobby Murdoch and John Clark. Front row – Stevie Chalmers, Willie Wallace, Jimmy Johnstone, Bobby Lennox and Bertie Auld

THE LISBON LIONS ARE TRUE Scottish football and sporting legends.

They have become as famous for their dentures as their glorious victory in the 1967 European Cup.

There was a fairytale element to this Celtic side who ended the Latin countries' dominance of the trophy.

All of Jock Stein's team were born within a thirty-mile radius of Celtic Park with all bar one – Bobby Lennox – hailing from within a ten-mile radius of the stadium. And after a breathtaking display of attacking football the team defeated the suntanned, Colgate-smiling players from Inter Milan.

Seconds after the final whistle was blown jubilant Celtic fans invaded the pitch and the goalkeeper Ronnie Simpson had to race back to his goal-mouth minutes later to retrieve his cap – which contained his false teeth and of those of some of his team-mates. The irony of this can't have been lost on right-back Jim Craig, who soon qualified as a dentist.

So, a famous victory for attacking football and the sugar-dominated Scottish diet that will never be equalled.

Therefore if a bunch of fat guys with no teeth – The Lisbon Lions – and an alcoholic from Fife, Jim Baxter, are genuine Scottish football legends then there is one Scotsman who combined their talents to become the archetypal Scottish sporting legend...

Jocky Wilson 40

JOCKY WILSON IS A FAT ALCOHOLIC FROM Fife with no teeth and winner of the Darts World Championship on two occasions in the 1980s. And probably the unlikeliest person to ever appear on Top of the Pops.

But believe it or not, he did!

Jocky reached the height of his fame when he won his first world title in 1982, the same year Dexy's Midnight Runners cover version of Van Morrison's *Jackie Wilson Said* reached number five in the UK charts.

When the band appeared on Top of the Pops, some chinless idiot straight out of university working on the show as a researcher (Can you believe that in the 1980s the BBC used to employ chinless idiots straight out of university as researchers?) thought the song was titled "Jocky Wilson Said".

Consequently, Dexy's performed the number (ok, mimed the number) in the TOTP studio in front of a giant screen bearing the image of a toothless guy from Kirkcaldy.

And people say the Eighties was a decade devoid of style.

Buoyed up by his new found status as a pop icon, when Jocky next won the World Title in 1989, he released a record of his own, *Jocky on the Oche*, but it failed to spark the public imagination and is reputed to have sold just 850 copies.

Jocky also courted controversy in 1982, due to his marriage to an Argentinian woman, Malvina, at the height of the Falklands War.

However it's amazing how short people's memories are. Because, in the summer of 1986, only four years later, the whole of Scotland worshipped the exploits of DIEGO MARADONA

Okay, he's from Argentina. But in that year's World Cup, he did score a goal against England with his hand. Enough said!

ANYONE OLD ENOUGH TO REMEMBER THE dreadful summer of 1978 will have had their memories scarred by the terrible low that was the World Cup in Argentina. The one glimmer of hope was provided by Archie Gemmill.

There may be better players to have worn the dark blue of Scotland but Archie Gemmill gave the nation hope at a time of despair.

He scored one of Scotland's greatest ever goals and one of the greatest solo goals in World Cup history.

Younger people will be familiar with Archie Gemmill's goal as it features very heavily in the storyline of the movie Trainspotting.

It was a marvellous solo effort of such poetic grace it was turned into a ballet.

More a *Nutmeg Suite* than a *Nutcracker Suite*.

Alas, Archie's brilliant goal was to no avail.

Scotland defeated eventual finalists Holland but not by enough goals to progress into the next round.

The team returned from Argentina and was hounded for failing so appallingly. Now Archie was blameless.

A lot of people blamed the tabloid press, a lot of people blamed the SFA, a lot of people blamed the players but mos people blamed manager Ally MacLeod.

That's unfair.

Yes, he made extravagant promises about how well his team would do but the euphoria was not created by MacLeod single-handedly. He was preaching to the converted. The nation loved his optimism.

For Scotland as a nation many commentators have ascribed the failure of the 1979 devolution referendum at least in part to the disastrous World Cup the year before.

But I don't think Ally MacLeod or any of the players shoul be blamed for the 1978 World Cup failure.

One man and one man alone should carry the can for tha campaign and that is Rod Stewart. His official World Cup song – *Olé Ola* - was a shocker.

The lyrics were essentially: *"Olé ola, olé ola – we're going to bring the World Cup back from over there."*

Shocking. How can a team wear the shirt with pride with

Archie Gemmill 39

ɑat as their official song?

Yet while at the time Argentina 1978 was considered ı utter fiasco, most fans today would swap that kind of iasco" with the current state of the game in Scotland. ever mind what happened when we got there. At least we ualified for the World Cup in 1978.

Football heroes have been thin on the ground in this untry in the 21st century.

But at least JAMES McFADDEN has continually inspired e nation and given us the chance to dream once again, no atter how briefly.

In the Euro 2004 play-off first leg, he scored the winner ainst Holland at Hampden Park. Sadly, in the second leg in nsterdam, Scotland lost 6-0.

In the 2010 World Cup qualifiers, he scored a solo goal orthy of Roy of the Rovers that clinched a 2-0 win over acedonia. Only for the Dutch to once more knock us out e next week.

But it was his exploits in the qualifying campaign for ro 2008, in particular his spectacular solo winning goal in Paris, that made the whole of Scotland believe we might qualify once again for a major tournament. For a brief time, we seemed to be walking on air, buoyed up by those dreams of success.

Then we all came crashing down to Earth again on a dreadful night in November 2007. Italy were awarded a dubious last-minute free-kick at Hampden Park, from which they inevitably scored the clinching goal.

Everyone's dreams were shattered, an entire nation was gutted, there seemed no point in going on any more. It was as if an enormous blanket of depression had descended upon the entire country from Berwick to Shetland. It was like being in a long dark tunnel without a chink of light at the end.

And this state of national depression went on for four whole days – until England were beaten by Croatia and suddenly life seemed alright once again. We are obtuse in Scotland in that we will never support the English at any sporting event.

But this is the awful dilemma we face when we don't qualify for a major tournament. For example, at the 2006 World Cup, England had qualified, we hadn't. So weird allegiances were formed.

A lot of Rangers fans supported Trinidad and Tobago, as they had a Trinidadian player at the time, Marvin Andrews. A number of Celtic fans supported Sweden out of loyalty to legendary ex-Celt Henrik Larsson. As chance would have it, Sweden played Trinidad at that World Cup.

Thankfully, the game ended in a draw. Otherwise, things could have got very messy in certain parts of Glasgow. Most Glaswegians are, after all, well aware of the ancient hatred that has long existed between the Trinidadians and the Swedes.

There was a rather unsavoury incident at the time of the 2006 World Cup, in Edinburgh of all places. In Inverleith Park, next to the middle-class suburb of Stockbridge, a seven-year-old English boy, wearing an England strip, was attacked by an older kid. Personally, I think the child was unlucky. The chances of meeting a Scottish person in that part of Edinburgh are pretty slim!

Tony Blair, however, felt compelled to issue a statement blaming the Tartan Army for the incident. But then Blair had clearly lost the plot entirely by the summer of 2006. However, attacking young children is not the behaviour of the Tartan Army. Any time Scotland qualify for the World Cup, the Tartan Army win the award for the best-behaved supporters at the tournament.

Mainly because we're not normally there long enough to start any trouble.

Blair's comments were not just ignorant. They were also irresponsible. Anything he said in 2006 would reach the ears of George W. Bush. So you can imagine how that retard would have reacted on hearing news about the Tartan Army attacking English people in the streets. He would have been looking in an atlas to find out where Tartania was so that he could invade us.

In fact, he probably had the CIA on the phone to him within hours:

"Mr President, it's worse than we thought. It's not just Tartania, it's Scotland as well. They've got chemical weapons in that country, sir. Even according to their own newspapers, they're developing a diabetes and heart-disease timebomb."

PERHAPS THE ONLY CHANCE SCOTLAND HAVE OF EVER winning a major tournament is to get the scientists at the Roslin Institute to use cloning technology to produce the Identikit Scottish Footballer...

The headbutting ability of Zinedine Zidane

The head of Joe Jordan

The perm of Alan Rough

The hand of Maradonna

The moustache of GraemeSouness

The heart of Dave Mackay

The stomach of Bobby Murdoch

The fingers of Allan McGregor

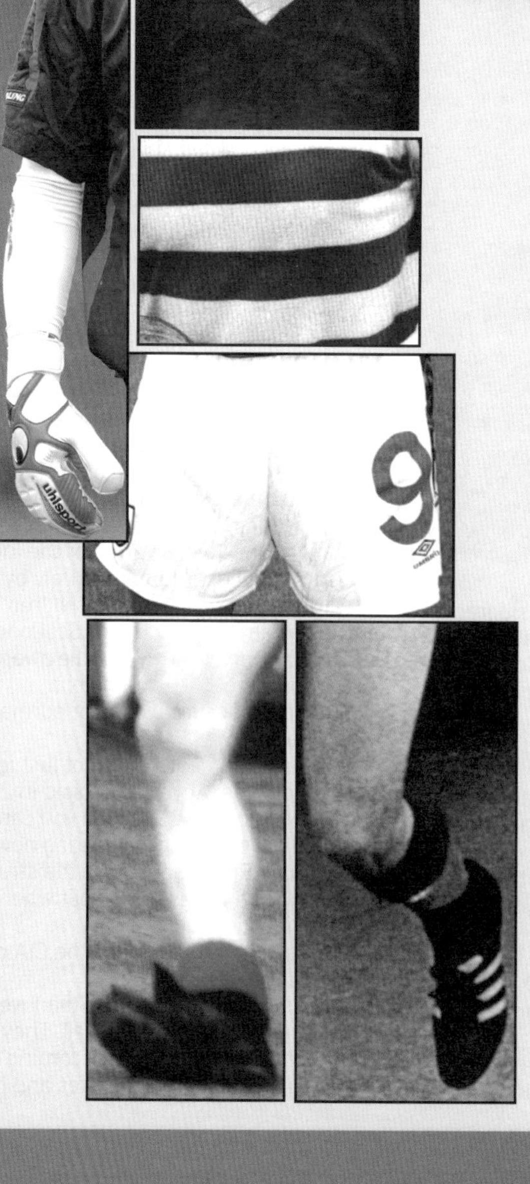

The groin of Frank McAvennie

The right foot of Jinky Johnstone

The left foot of Jim Baxter

Gordon Ramsay

NO ROOM IN THE IDENTIKIT Scottish footballer for Gordon Ramsay despite his short and glorious career with Glasgow Rangers – the glorious career he mentioned in his autobiography and in a series of interviews for press and radio.

However Ramsay's boasting of his football career was a complete pork pie. Admittedly a Michelin three-starred pork pie but a pork pie nonetheless. Ramsay had claimed to have played three competitive matches for Rangers.

But Rangers historian Robert McElroy– who has watched every competitive game the club has played since 1972 – claimed in March 2009 that Ramsay had never played a game for Rangers.

However, if any reader of this book can come up with documentary evidence that Gordon Ramsay ever played for Rangers, I will personally refund them the price of this book. And pay for a meal for two at one of his restaurants.

But Ramsay's place in this list is deserving for his two other talents swearing – although plenty of Scots could compete with him on that ability – and cooking.

As of 2009 he ranked third in the world in terms of Michelin Stars and this is a considerable achievement unlike *The F Word* on Channel 4.

Even with his dubious football career, Gordon Ramsay's change of career got me thinking - What if other ex-footballers became celebrity chefs?

Here are some recipe books we think should in the shops at Christmas...

BARRY FERGUSON

Finger Food

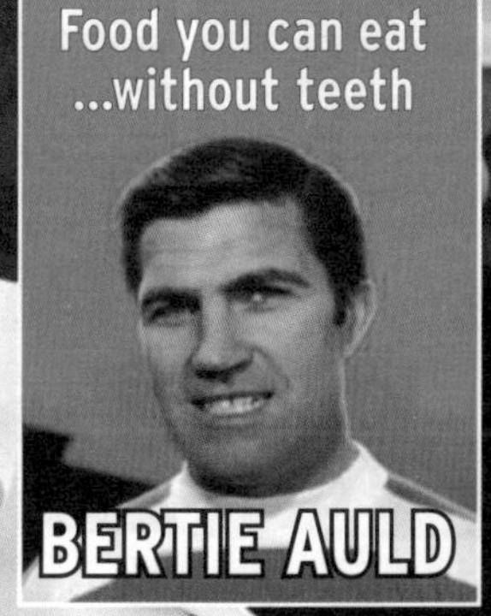

Food you can eat
...without teeth
BERTIE AULD

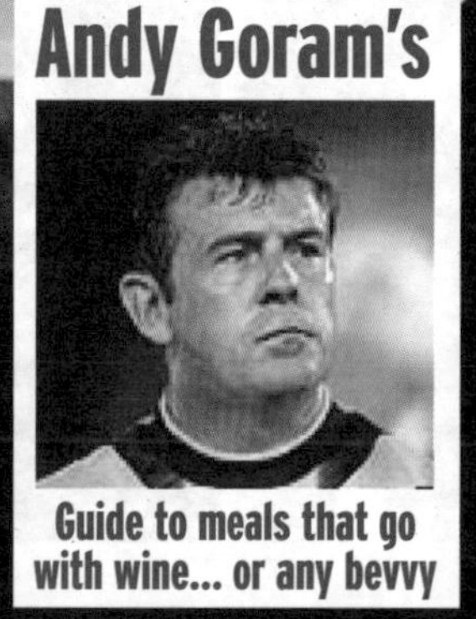

Andy Goram's
Guide to meals that go with wine... or any bevvy

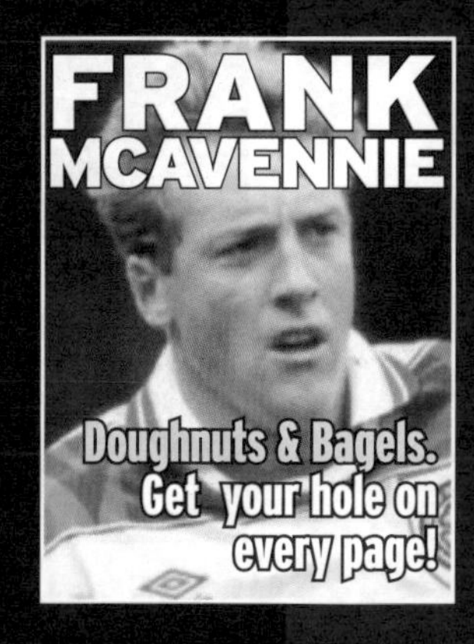

FRANK
MCAVENNIE
Doughnuts & Bagels.
Get your hole on every page!

WHEN CHUCK BERRY HEARD ROD STEWART'S cover of *Sweet Little Rock and Roller* he said, "Is this a white guy? You are kidding me." However, when most of us hear Rod Stewart speak, we similarly say, "Is this a Scottish guy? Are you kidding me?"

Born in the third-largest Scottish city (ie: London) Rod Stewart is perhaps the most famous Scotsman born in the big smoke.

But even allowing for that dreadful 1978 World Cup song, there is no denying Rod Stewart's influence on music worldwide.

He has sold more than 250 million albums and singles and performed in front of three-and-a-half million fans in one concert at Copacabana beach for Rio de Janeiro's 1994 New Year celebrations.

With his reputation for womanising perhaps it was no surprise he performed in front of so many Brazilians.

But this should come as no surprise as performers with Scottish parents have had a major impact on black musical culture.

Most recently MISS DYNAMITE. Born to a Hebridean mother and a Carribean father, an interesting cultural mix to say the least. One half Wee Free, the other half Rastafarian. Exactly how much mumbo-jumbo was she taught as a child?

GIL SCOTT-HERON – the poet, musician, and author had a Scottish mother. His father GIL HERON, was a professional footballer who played for Celtic in the 1950s.

The Scottish influence on Gil Scott-Heron is there for all to see. Alcoholic, drug addict, in and out of prison. You wonder why his dad bothered leaving the East End of Glasgow.

And, of course, there is BOB MARLEY.

The reggae superstar had a Jamaican mother but his white father was unknown to him however it is generally regarded his father was Scottish.

And when we face the fact that Bob Marley's dad got an 18 year-old knocked up and then virtually disappeared from any parental responsibilities – let's face it there is a good chance he was Scottish. Plus the fact that Bob Marley died of lung cancer... how much more proof do we need?

And then there is JOHN LENNON, who spent many childhood holidays in the North of Scotland. And in the 1970s crashed his Rolls-Royce in rural Caithness, while on a trip there with Yoko Ono, an event that has inspired an annual arts festival in the area.

And John Lennon was clearly heavily influenced by Scots culture. Apart from the obvious fondness for drink and drugs, Lennon was an opinionated trouble-maker with a permanent chip on his shoulder. He ended up being murdered. Pretty much the full set.

Also, the Scottish influence on country and western musi is undeniable.

NEIL GOW was the Perthshire fiddler who is credited wit developing – during the 1740s – the short bow saw stroke technique of playing the instrument.

And this fiddly-diddly musical style was exported to the Appalachian mountains which led to the invention of country and western music.

So we have a Scotsman to thank for all those songs abou misery, solitary drinking and domestic violence. Who'd hav thought?

And this country has not only produced rock stars but classical musicians too. Most notable recently NICOLA BENEDETTI, who first found chart success playing the violi at the age of 17.

The same year, Scotland on Sunday named her at numb 4 in their list of THE FIFTY MOST POWERFUL PEOPLE IN SCOTLAND. Jack McConnell was First Minister at the time, and was only listed at number 21.

Don't get me wrong, 21 was the correct position for Jack McConnell.

But for some lassie playing a violin to be considered the fourth most powerful person in Scotland? And you though this book's rating system was a bit random!

Liverpool Airport has now, of course, been named after John Lennon.

We think all of Scotland's airports could be re-named...

Rod Stewart

STORNOWAY: Donald Trump. Souvenir wigs on sale in shop. (Shop closed on Sundays)

GLASGOW: Tommy Sheridan. Strictly adults only. Have a relaxing tan before take-off

PRESTWICK: Elvis Presley. Who once spent half-an-hour there in 1958. And the locals have gone on and on and on and on and on about it ever since! Visit the memorial toilet

ATLANTIC OCEAN

Harris

Benbecula

Inve

SCO

Fort William

Gla

Ay

NORTHERN IRELAND

Belfast

Orkney
Thurso
Wick
Peterhead
Aberdeen
Dundee
Edinburgh
Lanark
Newcastle Upon Tyne
ENGLAND

INVERNESS: Charles Kennedy. Lots of amazing bargains on booze and fags in our duty free shop

DUNDEE: George Galloway. Direct flights to Baghdad. Have a relaxing tan before take-off

EDINBURGH: Sean Connery Pride of Scotland Airport. Direct flights to Spain, Barbados and all destinations where true patriots have relocated for tax purposes

36 The Krankies

THE KRANKIES ARE THE EMBODIMENT OF WHOLESOME family entertainment.

Quite incredible when you think about it.

Sixty-year-old married couple, she dresses up as a schoolboy.

Here they are in pantomime, she is dressed as schoolboy and he is dressed up as a woman. Later in the evening they give sweets away to children – and that is what they get up to in public.

What do they get up to in the privacy of their home?

Chic Murray 35

BILLY CONNOLLY IS WIDELY LAUDED AS THE greatest Scottish comedian of his generation. But even the Big Yin regards Chic Murray as the greatest Scots stand-up of all time.

With his ever-present bunnet perched on the side of his head, Chic Murray was one of the most recognisable faces to have emerged from Scotland and one of the finest comedians to have ever stood on a stage.

From Harry Lauder to Billy Connolly via Jimmy Logan, Stanley Baxter and Rikki Fulton, Scotland has a rich entertainment heritage. After all Stan Laurel's first stage appearance was in Glasgow. But Chic Murray was unique.

Chic was one of those rare old-time comedians who wrote his own material and it has seeped into the collective memory. His use of language was brilliant and ridiculously silly at the same time. "I made a stupid mistake last week. Come to think of it, did you ever hear of someone making a clever mistake?"

This comedic style is now commonplace in comedy clubs but then it was trailblazing. And it is not just fellow Scots who admire Murray's talent. In 2005 he was voted the comedian's comedian.

Here's why...

It's a small world, but I wouldn't want to have to paint it.

What use is happiness? It can't buy you money.

You know what they say about stamp collecting. Philately will get you nowhere.

The boat was so old; it must have been launched when Long John Silver had two legs and an egg on his shoulder.

My father was a simple man. My mother was a simple woman. You see the result standing in front of you, a simpleton.

There's a new slimming course just out where they remove all your bones. Not only do you weigh less, but you also look so much more relaxed.

I first met my wife in the tunnel of love. She was digging it at the time.

We were so poor; the ultimate luxury in our house at the time was ashtrays without advertisements.

I rang the bell of this small bed and breakfast place, whereupon a lady appeared at an outside window.
"What do you want?" she asked.
"I want to stay here," I replied.
"Well, stay there then," she said and closed the window.

I was in London the other day and this man came up to me and asked me if I knew the Battersea Dogs' Home. I said I didn't know it had been away.

If something's neither here nor there, where the hell is it?

David Byrne

DAVID BYRNE IS THE FORMER LEAD SINGER of Talking Heads, and their music was very much the sound track to the 1980s.

Talking Heads is of course an American band but David Byrne is Scottish – he was born in Dumbarton.

He emigrated to the States with his parents when he was a young child.

And one of their major hits of the 80s was Burning Down The House.

Here are the lyrics to that classic...

Watch out
You might get what you're after
Cool babies
Strange but not a stranger
I'm an ordinary guy
Burning down the house

Hold tight wait till the party's over
Hold tight were in for nasty weather
There has got to be a way
Burning down the house

Here's your ticket pack your bag: time for jumpin' overboard
The transportation is here
Close enough but not too far, maybe you know where you are
Fightin' fire with fire

All wet
Hey you might need a raincoat
Shakedown
Dreams walking in broad daylight
Three hundred sixty five degrees
Burning down the house

*Burning down the house**

This song is not just a soundtrack to the 1980s, but a soundtrack to the lives of many Scots, such as KENNY RICHEY.

A man who was on Death Row in the States for 17 years for a crime he didn't know if he committed or not.

He was accused of setting fire to a house where people died.

His defence was a straightforward one – he didn't know if he had committed the crime because he was pissed at the time.

And it's just not Kenny Richey.

Burning Down The House could also have been written for MIKE WATSON.

Watson was a former government minister who set fire to an hotel while drunk. He was sentenced to 16 months in prison.

Like Richey, Mike Watson could not remember what he had done (see also Number 19).

As his lawyer at court said: "This was an offence which was done without premeditation, motive, reason and indeed without recollection."

Another in this list, but he became a local hero, is SAKCHAI MAKAO.

In 2006 he was going to be deported back to Thailand from Shetland.

But Sakchai became a cause celebre and more than one-third of the island's population signed a petition demanding he stay in the UK.

His deportation order was overturned and he was allowed to stay on the Island.

Now the reason behind the UK government's attempt to deport him was that Sakchai had a criminal record for fire-raising while drunk.

Which I think helped him receive the backing of so many locals.

"Aye, he's one of us. He can light the wicker man the next time there is a visitor to the island."

If there is a theme to this section it is not to claim we are a nation of pyromaniacs but that we do have heavy drinking problem in this country.

There is no point in trying to pretend otherwise.

And the government is extremely concerned about this and in particular alcohol related diseases.

In fact they published a map of Scotland highlighting all the hotspots for all alcohol related illnesses in the country.

And with their kind permission we can reprint that map overleaf – all the hotspots are marked red on the map...

***Lyrics courtesy www.talking-heads.net**

OFFICIAL

Government map of Scottish hotspots for illnesses related to alcohol consumption

Buckfastleigh Abbey

A haven of rural solitude, where for centuries, the monks have been forbidden to communicate verbally. Where the strength of their faith is matched only by the quality of the refreshing and relaxing tonic wine brewed there.

Streets of Scotland

Looking out towards a scene of urban booze-related carnage, where each weekend many are unable to communicate verbally, due to the gargantuan consumption of a refreshing and relaxing tonic wine.

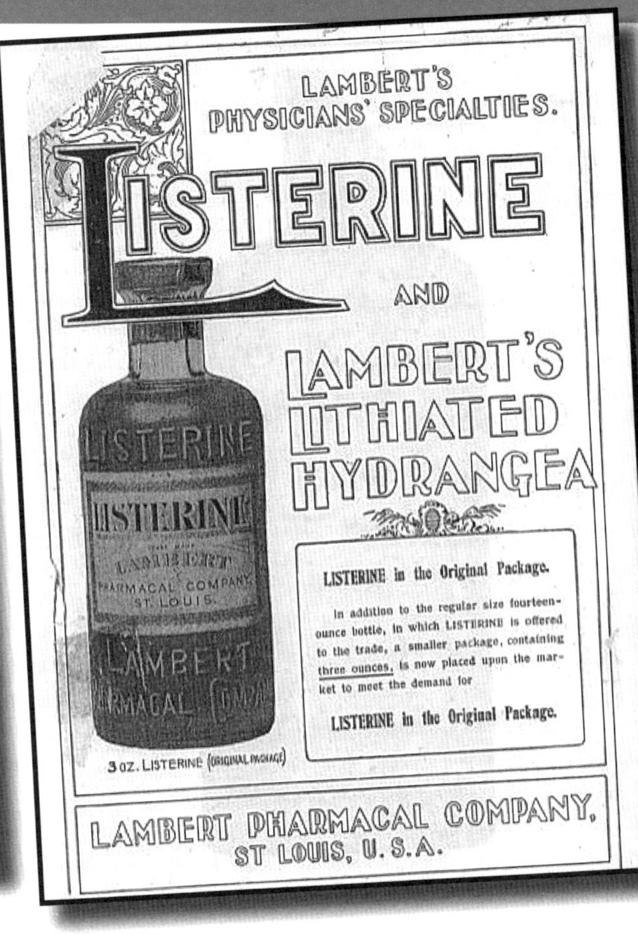

JOSEPH LISTER WAS A SURGEON WHO changed all our lives.

He was the man who created mouthwash.

In the 19th century Lister discovered the use of carbolic acid as an antiseptic and this became the first widely used antiseptic in surgery.

He has done more for the drugs industry over the years than Irvine Welsh.

Of course Lister wasn't actually Scottish – he was born and bred in Essex – but he lived in Scotland for a considerable period of his life and deserves his place in this list.

He is certainly regarded as a major contributor to Scotland's role in the progress of science and medicine.

Lister worked in both Glasgow and Edinburgh and was the professor of surgery at both cities' universities.

There is a statue in Glasgow's Kelvingrove Park celebrating his links with the city.

Lister's discovery of antiseptic isn't the only contribution the City of Glasgow has given to science.

In the 17th and 18th centuries, scales were developed by scientists to try to explain natural phenome Invariably, each natural phenomenon was one which occurred particularly frequently to the person devising th scale.

Hence THE BEAUFORT SCALE, to measure wind was formulated by Admiral Sir Henry Beaufort in the days of s Wind was important to him.

THE RICHTER SCALE, measuring the intensity of an

Joseph Lister

33

arthquake, was formulated by Prof Thomas Richter of the niversity of Southern California, where earthquakes are a ajor concern.

Likewise, the scale that measures the depth or intensity of coma is known as THE GLASGOW COMA SCALE.

This was formulated by doctors at Glasgow Royal firmary, who were having to deal with a variety of sorts of ma on a daily basis.

32 Andrew Carnegie

A MAN WHO ROSE FROM HUMBLE ORIGINS IN Fife, Andrew Carnegie became one of the USA's wealthiest men.

Building a business empire on steel, he owed much to the efforts of other people from humble origins.

A ruthlessly exploitative employer, he sent in armed troops to break up strikes.

However, he did redeem himself later in life by building a few libraries.

Another Scot who emigrated to the States, ALLAN PINKERTON, was the first-ever Private Eye, founding Pinkerton's, which is still the world's best-known detective agency. Who would have thought that someone from Edinburgh would have the idea of making money out of snooping into other people's affairs? Pinkerton was also Abraham Lincoln's bodyguard.

Hardly the most ringing endorsement.

Perhaps the two greatest technological innovations of the twentieth century, namely the invention of the telephone and the television, were the work of Scots.

I doubt whether either JOHN LOGIE BAIRD or ALEXANDER GRAHAM BELL could have imagined the enormous implications of their inventions.

JOHN LOGIE BAIRD IN PARTICULAR, must be spinning in his grave at what has happened to the medium he pioneered. Baird invented television in the 1930s as an alternative to sitting in the house doing nothing.

Whereas now, in the 21st century, people turn on their televisions specifically to watch people sitting in a house doing nothing.

So much modern television is mind-numbing dross.

Programmes like *Strictly Come Dancing*.

Who wants to see rugby players trying to become ballroom dancers?

Strictly Boxing

Joe Calzaghe takes on Michael Barrymore

It would be much better TV if the idea was the other way round, for example Bruce Forsyth scrumming down against the All Black front row.

It was another Scotsman, the redoubtably austere LORD REITH, who took stewardship of the BBC and ran the corporation under a strict code of conduct.

Presenters had to wear evening dress, and no one was employed to speak on the airwaves unless they could do so in the most refined of cut-glass accents.

A programme such as *Big Brother* could never have been broadcast in those days.

However, it is tempting to imagine what it might have been like...

John Logie Baird 31

WELCOME TO BIG BROTHER

PRESENTER: Here we are on the 37th day in the house

...Mr Ramsey-Palmer and the Honourable Lady Featherstonehaugh are in the lounge playing cribbage...

...Flight-Lieutenant Green is in the Diary Room...

GREEN: I would just like to say that Ramsey-Palmer is an utter stinker of he highest order. He had the absolute nerve to light his pipe at the dinner table in front of the Hon Lady Featherstonehaugh. I propose he should be kindly requested to leave the house.

PRESENTER: So, who would you like to be kindly requested to leave the house this week? The Hon Lady Featherstonehaugh, Mr Ramsey-Palmer or Flight-Lieutenant Green? Answers on a postcard, please, or telegrams by Friday morning.

AND, OF COURSE, IT WAS ANOTHER SCOTSMAN, albeit one who had long-since relocated to America, who invented the telephone.

Alexander Graham Bell and his assistant, Mr Watson, had been working on the technology for a long time before they carried out their final experiment...

Alexander Graham Bell 30

William Paterson

WILLIAM PATERSON FOUNDED THE BANK of England in 1694, before the Act of Union, to bankroll the English government.

He effectively invented modern banking as we know it.

And it was another Scot SIR FRED GOODWIN who effectively killed modern banking as we know it. A man who almost singlehandedly destroyed the Royal Bank of Scotland for which, ironically, it had to be bankrolled by the UK Government.

Despite losing £24 billion of shareholders' money, he still walked off with £8 million.

Although, in fairness to him, he did say he was sorry. Bizarrely, he seems okay at looking after his own money, but is careless with other peoples'.

He was briefly touted to succeed Max Moseley as head of Formula One. Presumably as he's the only person they could find who was sleazier than Moseley himself.

After all, who can replace the guy who fucked prostitutes in military garb better than a guy who fucked the whole UK banking sector?

A collective cheer could be heard throughout the UK on the day that Fred Goodwin's house in the Grange area of Edinburgh was vandalised.

Bricks were thrown through several of his windows, the kind of action that is normally met with disapproval in that part of the city.

This is the sort of neighbourhood where everyone is in Neighbourhood Watch.

But when his neighbours were interviewed about the incident, all these upstanding pillars of the Edinburgh middle-class establishment had to say to the press was: "You have to say, he had it coming. He's only got himself to blame."

However, there is one modern Scottish entrepreneur, who is seen in a much more positive light...

Duncan Bannatyne 28

BEST KNOWN TO THE PUBLIC AS ONE OF THE straight-talking no-nonsense "dragons" from TV's Dragons' Den, Duncan Bannatyne is the archetypal self-made millionaire.

Having been discharged from the Navy and after a spell in prison, he set himself up in business with an ice cream van.

He then went on to amass a personal fortune, through developing care homes for the elderly and fitness centres.

But it's as a patron of new inventors that he is best loved.

Bannatyne represents all that is best in the twin Scots traditions of business and innovation. He uses his own personal wealth to encourage and support the innovation of others.

I have a number of inventions on the drawing board which I would like to take to Dragons' Den.

The first is the Acme Drinking Helmet. Similar in design to the headgear worn by American footballers, but made of soft rubber, it would enable the wearer to fall over, walk into doors or indeed receive a severe kicking in a street fight without injury.

The visor would be replaced by a tray device large enough to hold a kebab or a portion of chips. A drinking tube attached to an inbuilt water supply would protect against overnight de-hydration.

It would come supplied with satnav, which could be programmed to direct the wearer home, or to the toilet.

In order to be fully effective, the helmet should be worn in conjunction with the Acme Corrective Boot.

This has to be fitted by a podiatrist who must first accompany the would-be wearer on a drinking session, to assess their gait when drunk.

Once they have established which foot the client favours when suffering from wobbly-boot syndrome, a weighted corrective boot is then fitted to the other foot.

Duke of Sutherland

UNDOUBTEDLY ONE OF THE MOST evil monsters in the entire history of Scotland, the Duke of Sutherland was one of the landowners who instigated the Highland Clearances from the mid-1700s onwards.

The crofters' cottages were burned down, they were herded into boats and sent across the Atlantic to Canada, in order to clear their homeland for sheep.

If that wasn't bad enough, he then forced his few remaining tenants to erect an enormous statue of him at the top of the highest hill for miles around. Amazingly, it still stands to this day. In most other countries of the world it would have been blown up by now, and rightly so.

The Highland Clearances must go down as one of the bleakest periods in Scottish history. Indeed, only one event can surpass its catastrophic nature. And that is England winning the World Cup in 1966.

If you don't believe me. Ring any Scotsman's doorbell tomorrow morning and give them a choice. You're going to burn their house down and send them off on a boat to Canada, or England win the World Cup. Ninety-nine per cent will choose to go to Canada.

After all, you can always come back from Canada. And at least the BBC didn't film the Highland Clearances and repeatedly show it on TV for the next forty-odd years.

2009 saw the promotion of a major cultural festival, Homecoming Scotland. The idea behind this nationwide series of events was to encourage ex-pat Scots to return home.

Thus it featured a parade of massed pipes and drums in Edinburgh, with as many as a million bagpipers. It also included the largest Highland Games ever to be organised anywhere in the world and an enormous Gathering of the Clans. In other words all the things they left Scotland to get away from in the first place.

Now, I am aware that not all expats, or more accurately their forebears, had a choice as to whether they left these shores or not. But have these people not suffered enough already?

Two hundred years after their ancestors' cottages were burned down, and they were dispatched on boats to Canada, to drag these people back over the Atlantic once more to subject them that kind of shit was gratuitously sadistic.

William of Orange

MANY OUTSIDERS HAVE INFLUENCED Scotland's history and culture. None more so than William of Orange. Indeed, over three hundred years after the Battle of the Boyne, his followers still march through streets of Glasgow in an open act of religious intolerance.

However, the Loyal Orange Order of Scotland, who organise the Orange Parades apparently want to re-brand the Twelfth of July and market it as an international festival to attract tourists. What kind of demented person is going to consider that to be a holiday?

While there are doubtless a few flute enthusiasts out there who might be attracted by the event, I suggest the most fruitful course of action would be to market the Twelfth of July as an extreme holiday for gap-year students.

The kind of people who get 'awfully excited' by going to Pamplona for the Running of the Bulls...

FLIGHTS FROM
MAJOR UK AIRPORTS
ALL ARRIVE AT 16:90
VISIT
GLASGOW
This July...
enjoy the
running of
the bigots,
bands,
& Buckfast
HIRE A
BASS DRUM
WEAR A
BOWLER
ADRIAN, 22, FROM HENLEY SAYS:
'Tarquin was up to his knees in Fenian blood. It was bloody fantastic!'

Bubbling under: Part 1

WE'RE HALFWAY THROUGH THE TOP OF OUR Hit Parade of the Greatest Scots of All Time Ever!

So we should briefly take some time to mention those who are bubbling under the charts but didn't quite make it into our Top 50.

BARACK OBAMA

THE SCOTTISH DIASPORA COVERS virtually the entire globe.

Many Scots throughout the world are proud of their heritage. Almost all of them are aware of their roots. To some, however, their Scottishness comes as a complete surprise.

Barack Obama, for example, only found out about his Caledonian ancestry on November 5th 2008 when he received a telegram from Alex Salmond congratulating him on being the fifth US President with Scottish roots.

Obama is reported to have been so stunned by the news that he immediately went out and got pissed.

The reaction to Obama's election Stateside was unlike anything we have witnessed here. Over a million people descended on Washington for the inauguration. Or, the previous day, when he took his train journey from Phildelphia to Washington in the footsteps of Lincoln, there were thousands of delirious fans on every platform waiting to greet him.

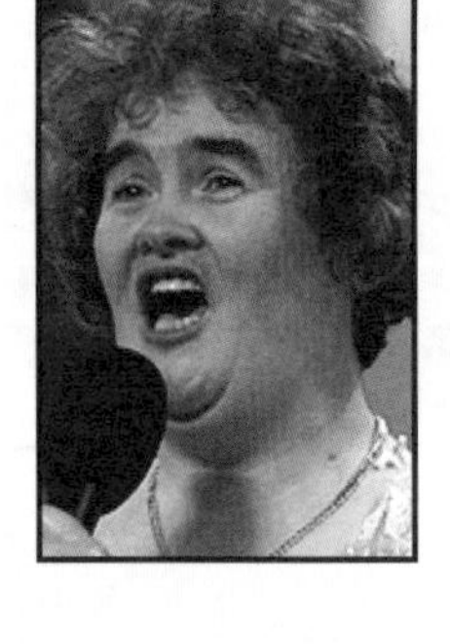

That would never have happened in Britain. Imagine when Gordon Brown took power if he had taken a train from Kirkaldy down to London. He would have been met by a handful of half-hearted souls en route, while half-a-dozen people were waiting at Kings Cross Station to hear the inevitable tannoy announcement: "We apologise for the late running of the Prime Minister's train. This is due to essential engineering work in the Stevenage area. The Prime Minister will now be arriving on a replacement bus service from Peterborough."

Obama and Brown do share some things in common. For example they both have a catchphrase. Obama's is "Yes, we can".

Brown's is "Sorry".

KENNY MacASKILL

KENNY MACASKILL FEATURES elsewhere in this book. But it is worth mentioning him here, while we are on the subject of the Scottish diaspora.

In 2009 the Scottish Government launched the Homecoming Festival, aimed at attracting ex-pats back from abroad. Particularly from North America. This is a similar initiative to Tartan Week, held annually in New York City, which tries to tempt Americans to invest in Scotland.

Kenny MacAskill's added to these overtures to the USA by releasing the Lockerbie bomber!

When al-Megrahi was taken up the steps of his plane at Glasgow Airport, it was obvious John Smeaton was not at work that day. He would have been chasing him round the terminal building shouting "Cancer, you say? I'll soon kick yer fucking cancer out of you!"

SUSAN BOYLE

ONE SCOT WHO HAS, HOWEVER, captured the hearts of the American people is Blackburn's very own Susan Boyle.

It really is amazing how she has become a global star.

Indeed, she went from nowhere to the Priory Clinic in the space of about two months. That takes some doing. Most people squeeze a career into the middle. But not our Susan. The pressure of singing two songs was so great she had to be booked into rehab.

She has of course now had a makeover. Or shave, as we should more accurately term it. And it must be said, she's not at all bad-looking by West Lothian standards.

NICOLA STURGEON

ANOTHER POLITICIAN WHO FAILED to make it into our Top Fifty is Nicola Sturgeon, despite her high profile as Scotland's Minister for Swine Flu.

The one thing the Government knows about Swine Flu is that the Government knows the Government knows fuck-all about Swine Flu.

Advice and information change on an almost daily basis.

We are told Swine Flu is unlikely to be fatal, unless the victim happens to be overweight, diabetic, a heavy smoker or suffers from a heart condition. In other words, it could wipe out half of Scotland in a matter of months.

And, of course, it is all the fault of us, the public. Because we haven't been sneezing properly.

I must admit I am very grateful to the Government for their "Catch It, Bin It, Kill It" advertisements on TV, as until then I hadn't a clue how to sneeze.

Personally, I can't wait for an outbreak of diarreah. I expect the Government to put adverts on the telly, informing of the correct way to wipe my arse: "Shite It, Wipe It, Don't Bite It !!"

BUBBLING UNDER PART 2: PAGE 88

St Andrew

ST ANDREW: THE PATRON SAINT OF Scotland.

After he was crucified, Andrew's followers were instructed to make sure his bones were safe.

They were told it was imperative to take his remains to the ends of the earth.

So St Andrew's bones were placed into a boat and taken to the ends of the earth and in those days that happened to be Fife.

Fife may no longer be the ends of the earth, but it still is the best place to go in the English-speaking world to listen to people swearing.

I once overheard a conversation in Kirkcaldy, where one guy called another guy a 'cunty-pussed-fuck-wank'.

Which is more than swearing, it is bordering on poetry.

St Andrew was not Scottish, yet we now consider him to be one of our own.

In much the same way, we consider...

24 Mary Queen of Scots

...MARY QUEEN OF SCOTS: Queen of Scotland. Though she was French.

But she took the Scots to her heart. And to other parts of her body if history is to be believed.

Mary's easy morals were at odds, however with her nemesis...

John Knox

The Editor
Stornoway Gazette

Dear Sir,
Being someone who is actively engaged in the writing, speaking and use of the Gaelic language on a daily basis I find it deeply lamentable that the powers that be in the broadcasting fraternity agree to the transmission of Gaelic television programmes on the Sabbath at the very time 6.10 pm that it is the duty of each and everyone of us to be at the Means of Grace on Sabbath evening.

I am conscious bound to remind the Media Community and anyone else reading this letter, of their duty to uphold that part of the moral law, contained in Exodus Chapter 20 verses 8-11. The day is fast approaching when each and everyone of us shall be required to sit at the judgement seat of Christ, believer and non-believer alike.

As scripture doth remind us the Fourth Commandment to keep Holy the Sabbath Day is no less binding than any of the other commandments, for example Adultery, Murder, Theft and Bearing False Witness contained in God's Holy Law Unless our sins be washed in the blood of the Lamb, We shall leave this world in an unregenerate and condemned state.

Yours etc...

...WHO WAS, OF COURSE, OSAMA bin Laden. No, this is actually John Knox.

However, the similarity is frightening.

I call this look "religious fundamentalist chic". And the comparisons between Knox and bin Laden are not superficial.

Immediately after the Reformation, Scotland was run by a regime not a million miles removed from the Taliban, the country governed under a code of strict religious rule.

That may seem strange when one considers the modern-day Church of Scotland, one of the most liberal, open-minded and humanitarian of Western faiths.

Yet the spirit of Knox lives on in the 21st century in the form of the Free Presbyterian Church, the Taliban of Christianity whose homeland is the Western Highlands and Islands.

In order to gain an insight into the "Wee Free" mentality it is helpful to read their local papers. In particular THE STORNOWAY GAZETTE.

In particular the letters page of the Stornoway Gazette.

Above is an actual letter that appeared in that newspaper's pages as recently as 2005,

The thing about that letter is that it's about TV scheduling. Christ knows what reaction you would get if you were to propose opening a gay sauna.

Stornoway was, however, at the centre of one of the most heart-warming examples of multi-culturalism in recent years.

It centred around 15-year-old Molly Campbell, who chose to live with her father in Pakistan rather than her mother in Stornoway. A difficult decision to make at that age.

On one hand, you can live in a far-flung outpost of the British Empire, where people are struggling to come to terms with the 21st century, their lives ruled by religious fundamentalism.

And on the other hand, you can live in Pakistan.

22 Bonnie Prince Charlie

BONNIE PRINCE CHARLIE AND FLORA MacDonald were basically, a gay man and a fag hag.

It says much about the anti-English sentiment at the time that the Jacobites were prepared to put their ingrained homophobia to one side.

Their logic was that they'd prefer a French poof to an Englishman, as they assumed the Englishman would be a poof in any case. Even if he wasn't gay.

What did Charlie get out of it?

He got to wear a kilt.

A hobby of French homosexuals right up until present-day examples such as JEAN-PAUL GAULTIER.

John Smeaton 21

JOHN SMEATON IS THE HERO FROM THE summer of 2007 for his act of derring-do at Glasgow Airport - kicking a burning terrorist in the groin.

Doesn't that just sum up the unacceptable levels of violence that the people of the West of Scotland have become accustomed to.

Only in Glasgow can being on fire be no protection for getting attacked.

Of course the man on fire was one of the two terrorists who had just driven a burning car full of propane gas canisters into the airport terminal building.

Smeaton was a 31-year-old baggage handler who just happened to be outside on his fag break.

It was a triumph for the human spirit.

It was a triumph for the Scottish notion of fair play.

And it was a triumph for the smoking ban.

The reason he was so instantly loved by the Scottish public is that he expressed, in words and actions, values we like to think are characteristics in the DNA of all Scots: Namely courage, selflessness, modesty and lets face it being hard as nails in the face of danger.

Furthermore, Smeaton's interviews were hilarious, vividly told with a full range of hammy acting skills.

When asked by BBC News to describe the burning car, he poetically replied: "Anyone who's ever thrown a lit can of deodorant on a bonfire will know exactly what it's like."

But John Smeaton is actually an interesting guy - virtually a modern fairytale.

Think how his life has changed since that day.

His lifestyle exploded like that proverbial lit can of deodorant thrown onto a bonfire.

Not long ago he was just a normal 31-year-old working class guy who lived with his parents.

Now he is an international celebrity, and all because he'd popped outside for a quick fag...

ALEX SALMOND HAS PRETTY MUCH AVOIDED BEING directly implicated in any major scandal, letting Justice Minister Kenny MacAskill take most of the flak for the Lockerbie bomber's release.

Yet, when examining his record in office, it is interesting to note who Salmond's major funders are.

They include SIR TOM FARMER, a right-wing tyre-and-exhaust tycoon and devout Catholic.

The man who founded then sold off Kwik-Fit, who has been honoured by both Margaret Thatcher and The Pope.

The man who now owns Hibernian FC.

And then there is another leading Scottish businessman - BRIAN SOUTER - the transport tycoon, and founder of Stagecoach.

Both Farmer and Souter can both be viewed as members of the Road Lobby.

One of Salmond's first acts in government was to remove all road tolls in Scotland. I am not suggesting for one minute that this is corrupt. It just happens to be the way that politics works, and always has done.

For example, Britain's railway infrastructure was decimated in the early 1960s when Ernest Marples was Transport Secretary. The same Ernest Marples, who was a director of Marples Ridgway, the construction company responsible for building much of the UK's motorway network.

Obviously, a complete coincidence.

There was, however, a hint of scandal in the air when Salmond intervened in the affairs of Donald Trump (See Number 18).

Swept to power by the decisive mandate of 30% of the popular vote in the 2007 election, where a stunning 100,000-plus spoiled ballots were recorded, Alex has spent the subsequent time in power doing what he does best - blaming the English for everything.

Indeed, the 2007 Scottish parliamentary election was a watershed in our nation's history. It not only delivered us our first Nationalist administration, but it also represented a pinnacle of incompetent behaviour in the history of the Scottish political classes. In particular it showed up the incompetence of New Labour north of the Border.

To organise a ballot paper that completely confused the voters is bad enough. To do so and then lose the election is inefficiency on a farcical scale.

Passions rose so high that on the night of the 2007 election a voter in Edinburgh attacked a polling station wielding a golf club. What a particularly Edinburgh way of making your feelings felt!

In Paisley or Dundee, he would have used a baseball bat.

I like to think it was some disaffected Tory voter, being egged-on by his like-minded mates at the 19th Hole.

Hamish: "I tell you, Finlay, there's absolutely no point in voting Conservative in this bloody country any more. A bit of direct action's what we need.

Finlay: Give these effing Socialists a taste of their own medicine.

Hamish: What are you doing taking a putter with you, Finlay?

Finlay: This is a job for a mashie, old chap!"

The SNP Government came to power with a number of pledges. One was an end to the building of new nuclear power stations north of the Border.

I personally believe that we have no need of nuclear power in a country as rich as Scotland is in natural resources. We can harness the energy of the wind, the tides and the mountains.

It has often been claimed that Scotland could become 'The Saudi Arabia of Renewable Energy'.

And indeed we could.

We have wind farms, we have developed ground-breaking technology in tidal power, we have hydro-electric.

We have the capability to produce solar energy on at least three days each year.

It is simply a question of harnessing our resources to create energy.

We also have a lot of high mountains and a lot of obese young people. It has been suggested by a team of scientists that a generator could be sited at the top of Ben Nevis, with a bungee cord attached to it.

All that remains is to tie Michelle McManus to the other end and then push her off the top.

It has been estimated that this could generate enough electricity to power the entire Lochaber area for about a month.

There does remain the nagging question of how Michelle McManus can be taken up to the top of Ben Nevis in the first place.

A focus group came up with the suggestion of opening a branch of Gregg's the bakers at the summit.

The SNP has also promised the people of Scotland a referendum on independence. Which, if nothing else, will brin the argument to a conclusion.

It is somewhat naïve to think that a referendum in itself wil deliver independence.

Students of history will know that the British Empire does not always give away colonies that easily. America had to fight a war of independence. Ireland had to fight a war of independence. Indian independence was brought about largely because Ghandi went on hunger strike to bring down the British Raj.

You can hardly see Alex Salmond going on a hunger strike!

There are other routes to independence. In some countries, people have set themselves on fire to attract support for their cause, such as Jan Palak i Czechoslovakia in 1968.

In Scotland, this will only earn you a severe kicking from a passing baggage handler (See John Smeaton, Number 21).

Independence could be gained by fighting a war.

Obviously it wouldn't be started by the Scots.

It would be caused by US and British military intelligence finding evidence of weapons of mass destructior in Scotland.

Because there are plenty of weapons of mass destruction in Scotland. All of them put there by the Americans and the British.

Funnily enough, I quite fancy Scotland's chances at this or

After all, if the British are going to be stupid enough to leave their nuclear weapons in Scotland...

Or, we could win independence by the means of a penalty shoot-out. Against England!

That would be a shoo-in for the Scots.

From a Nationalist perspective, if Alex Salmond is genuine serious about delivering independence he should insist on a UK-wide vote.

If the English people get a say on the matter, Scotland cou be independent within months rather than years.

New Labour - surprise, surprise - are divided by the referendum issue. Gordon Brown is against the idea.

Many in Scotland including former leader WENDY ALEXANDER are in favour.

The only way forward is for New Labour to hold a referendum about whether we are to have a referendum.

Those who remember the Alexander Brothers as the personification of showbiz naffness in the 1970s will recogn the work of Wendy and DOUGLAS ALEXANDER as their political reincarnation.

Wendy had to resign for taking inappropriate funding for leadership election in which she was elected unopposed.

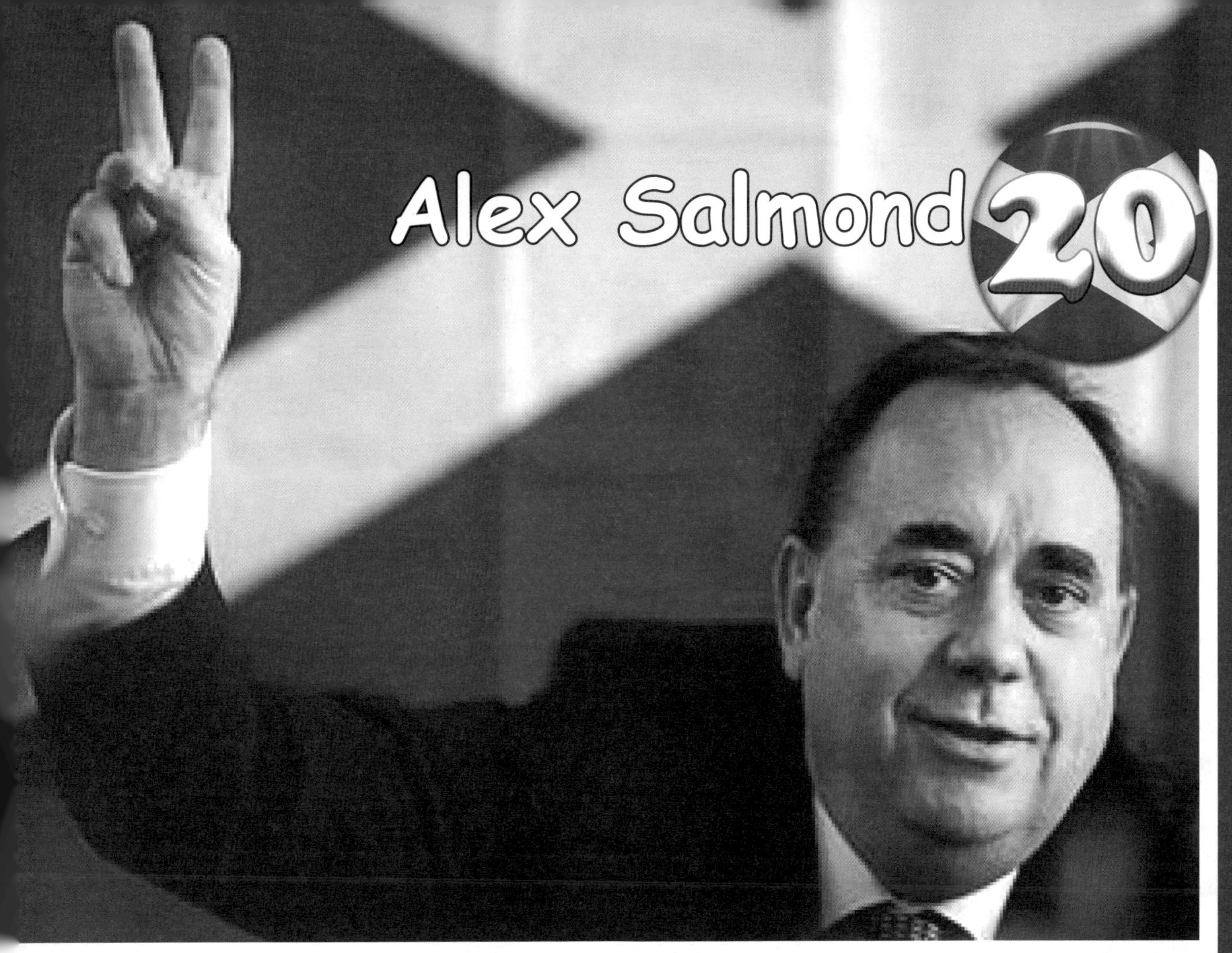

And she's the bright one of the family.

Douglas was the brains behind the utterly confusing 2007 ballot paper.

His next job was Overseas Development Secretary, in which position he had the nerve to criticise Robert Mugabe's handling of the Zimbabwean election.

So, Wendy may have been playing a smart game, even from a Unionist perspective.

My guess is that she was hoping that the referendum would be run from London, and that her brother would be given the job of running it.

Following his spectacular success in 2007, Douglas Alexander could no doubt make an even bigger balls-up of this one.

Here is an illustration of the logical way to a design a ballot paper...

Should Scotland be independent?

YES ☐

NO ☐

Please place a cross in the appropriate box.

However, a Douglas Alexander-designed referendum ballot paper might read like this:

Should Scotland be independent?

YES go to question 2

NO go to question 2

MAYBE go to Berwick-upon-Tweed

Question 2 How independent should Scotland be or not be?
Please place a number in the boxes alongside in order of preference. (Or, if you don't fancy that idea, just put a cross anywhere on the paper)

1 Very independent
2 Independent
3 Quite independent
4 Sort of half-way between independent and not independent
5 Not independent
6 Not independent at all
7 Haven't a Scooby
8 Haven't a fucking clue
9 What's independent mean, pal?
10 Can I go now, please?

Cue confusion on a national scale, widespread panic, a rise in fuel prices (any excuse will do) and irate Edinburgh voters rampaging round polling stations wielding golf clubs.

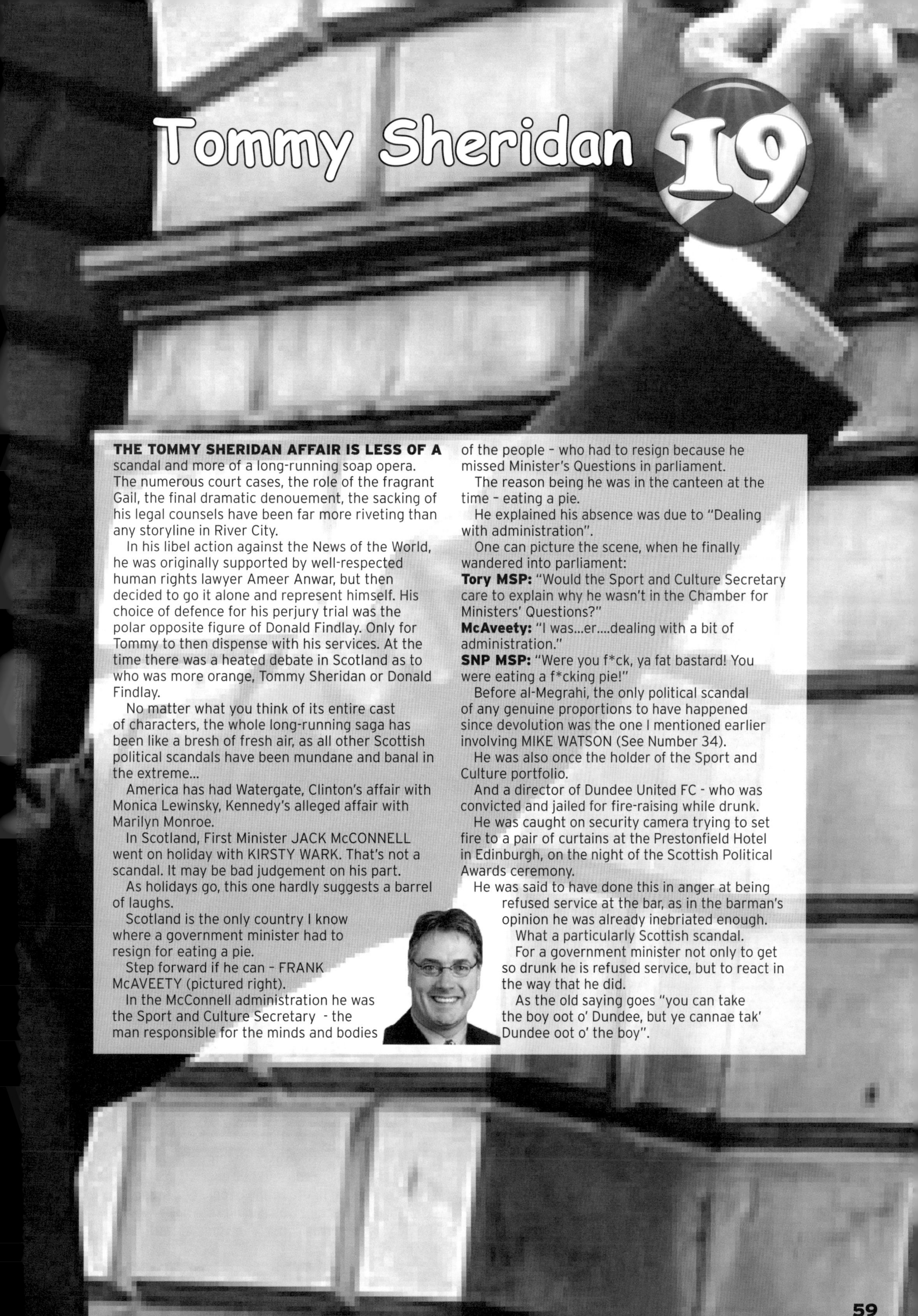

Tommy Sheridan 19

THE TOMMY SHERIDAN AFFAIR IS LESS OF A scandal and more of a long-running soap opera. The numerous court cases, the role of the fragrant Gail, the final dramatic denouement, the sacking of his legal counsels have been far more riveting than any storyline in River City.

In his libel action against the News of the World, he was originally supported by well-respected human rights lawyer Ameer Anwar, but then decided to go it alone and represent himself. His choice of defence for his perjury trial was the polar opposite figure of Donald Findlay. Only for Tommy to then dispense with his services. At the time there was a heated debate in Scotland as to who was more orange, Tommy Sheridan or Donald Findlay.

No matter what you think of its entire cast of characters, the whole long-running saga has been like a bresh of fresh air, as all other Scottish political scandals have been mundane and banal in the extreme...

America has had Watergate, Clinton's affair with Monica Lewinsky, Kennedy's alleged affair with Marilyn Monroe.

In Scotland, First Minister JACK McCONNELL went on holiday with KIRSTY WARK. That's not a scandal. It may be bad judgement on his part.

As holidays go, this one hardly suggests a barrel of laughs.

Scotland is the only country I know where a government minister had to resign for eating a pie.

Step forward if he can – FRANK McAVEETY (pictured right).

In the McConnell administration he was the Sport and Culture Secretary - the man responsible for the minds and bodies of the people – who had to resign because he missed Minister's Questions in parliament.

The reason being he was in the canteen at the time – eating a pie.

He explained his absence was due to "Dealing with administration".

One can picture the scene, when he finally wandered into parliament:

Tory MSP: "Would the Sport and Culture Secretary care to explain why he wasn't in the Chamber for Ministers' Questions?"

McAveety: "I was...er....dealing with a bit of administration."

SNP MSP: "Were you f*ck, ya fat bastard! You were eating a f*cking pie!"

Before al-Megrahi, the only political scandal of any genuine proportions to have happened since devolution was the one I mentioned earlier involving MIKE WATSON (See Number 34).

He was also once the holder of the Sport and Culture portfolio.

And a director of Dundee United FC - who was convicted and jailed for fire-raising while drunk.

He was caught on security camera trying to set fire to a pair of curtains at the Prestonfield Hotel in Edinburgh, on the night of the Scottish Political Awards ceremony.

He was said to have done this in anger at being refused service at the bar, as in the barman's opinion he was already inebriated enough.

What a particularly Scottish scandal.

For a government minister not only to get so drunk he is refused service, but to react in the way that he did.

As the old saying goes "you can take the boy oot o' Dundee, but ye cannae tak' Dundee oot o' the boy".

18 Donald Trump

THE AMERICAN BILLIONAIRE DONALD TRUMP, famous for his skyscrapers has a Scottish mother. Alex Salmond's government intervened in his planning application to build a huge golfing resort in Aberdeenshire.

After the local council had turned down the application, it was approved by the Scottish government.

However, it's stretching credibility to suggest that back-handers were on offer.

Donald Trump may be immensely rich and just as powerful, but he does come across as being very tight-fisted. Someone with his millions, yet who refuses to buy a decent wig, is not going to be handing out bribes willy-nilly.

The Trump comb-over may, of course, have been suggested by image consultants, eager to make him a more appealing figure to the people of Scotland.

"Mr Trump, we think you should take on the look of a Scottish cultural icon. We've come up with this guy here..."

Archie Macpherson 17

....THE LEGENDARY FOOTBALL commentator and broadcaster Archie Macpherson.

Trump has reputedly hired a voice coach, who insists on him repeating one word: "Woof!"

Introduced by
ARCHIE MACPHERSON

16 David Livingstone

SOME SCOTS LEFT THE shores of the homeland of their own accord. Some in search of a better life for themselves. Some because they believed that they could better the lives of others.

David Livingstone was one of the latter. Originally a hand-loom weaver from Lanarkshire, he trained in medicine and became a medical missionary in Africa, dedicating his life to working with the poor.

He founded a town in Malawi, Blantyre, which he named after his home town in Scotland.

To this day, there have been strong links between Malawi and Scotland. Jack McConnell visited Blantyre, Malawi, while he was First Minister. And in a laughable photo opportunity, was made a tribal chief.

What was particularly risible was the fact that at the time, First Minister or not, McConnell could have walked down the Main Street in Blantyre, Lanarkshire, without anyone knowing who the hell he was.

Until someone pointed him out as the man who had stopped us from smoking in the pub.

Then he'd have to run for cover.

David Hume

A RADICAL PHILOSOPHER FROM THE 1700s, David Hume's impact upon academics and intellectuals remains as powerful now as it did three centuries ago.

His influence at the time was enormous, and his work is still studied by philosophy students throughout the world.

Hume declared: "We will not improve the human condition by fear of God. We will only improve the human condition by the application of reason."

An astonishingly radical statement to make in a time when religious dogma was followed by the majority of people without question.

There is a statue of David Hume on Edinburgh's Royal Mile – more often than not with a traffic cone on his head.

I like to think that the traffic cone has been placed there by philosophy students from Edinburgh University after a night on the bevvy having just read one of his books.

As they drop the traffic cone onto the head of the statue I imagine the students declaring: "We will only improve the condition of this statue by the application of this traffic cone."

Hume was years ahead of his time. In 1745 he published a book in which he laid down various guidelines which would lead to an improvement in the living conditions of his fellow Scots.

These were:

- **RESPECT FOR WOMEN**
- **KINDNESS TO CHILDREN**
- **BETTER HOUSING**
- **LESS DRINKING**
- **LESS FIGHTING**
- **A BETTER DIET**

That was in 1745. How much has changed since then?

Greyfriars Bobby

THERE ARE MANY STATUES THROUGHOUT Edinburgh underlining the city's rich cultural history.

And yet one of the most popular is that of a dog - Greyfriars Bobby. What a heart-warming tale.

Greyfriars Bobby was a terrier dog who remained by his master's grave for 14 years.

Assuming that the dog wasn't still on its lead you have to conclude that Greyfriars Bobby was either a bit thick or a bit creepy - hanging around a graveyard for 14 years.

This was during the Victorian era and a cemetery was a safe place for a dog to hang around unaccompanied. Couldn't do that nowadays.

No dog could hang around a graveyard for 14 days never mind 14 years without some ned ramming a firework up its arse.

Graveyards are no longer the resting place of the deceased. They've become a playground for young hooligans. There was an infamous case in 2004 when a teenager broke into Greyfriars Cemetery and dug up a corpse. And as he did so, the corpse's head fell off.

Now this would freak most people out but this youngster wasn't fazed by this at all.

In fact he used the skull as a ventriloquist's dummy and displayed his football skills by playing keepy-uppy with it.

And then, in the words of the Daily Record, performed a lewd sex act on it. As though there is any other sex act you can perform on a corpse.

When he was found guilty of violation of a sepulcher - yes, that is still a crime in Edinburgh - the judge sentenced him to community service. Ironically cleaning up graveyards.

The major mistake the youth made was timing.

He broke in to the cemetery in January. If he had done this in August during the Festival Fringe he would have won an award.

Returning to Greyfriars Bobby, it is worth noting that the City of Edinburgh gave the terrier the freedom of the city.

Yes, they gave the freedom of the city to a dog.

Glasgow - so often looked down upon by some Edinburgh residents - gave the freedom of their city to Nelson Mandela.

Burke & Hare

IF YOU ARE GIVING OUT THE freedom of the city for not leaving graveyards then you'd be as well giving the freedom of the city to Burke and Hare, the notorious grave robbers who spent plenty of time in cemeteries.

All they have to commemorate them is a pub, the *Burke and Hare*.

Ironically, the pub named after two body snatchers is now a lap-dancing bar.

Similarly, Deacon Brodie was a notorious thief who was sent to the gallows.

There is a pub named after him. Likewise, *The Maggie Dickson* pub celebrates a woman who

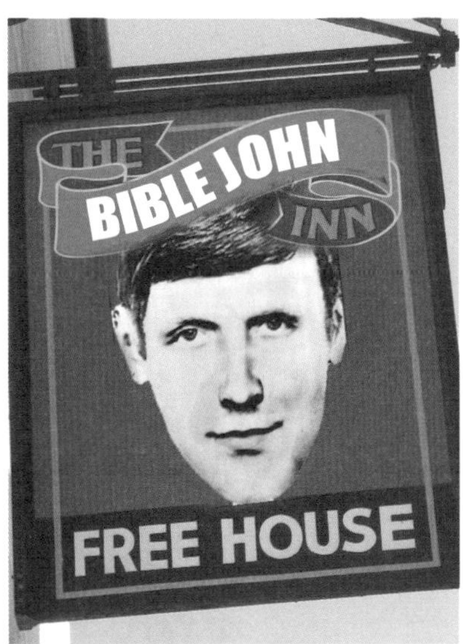

was hanged at the gallows but survived.

What is it about the city of Edinburgh that they name pubs after criminals and murderers?

Does some decent period of time have to elapse before a you can name a pub after a notorious criminal?

"Do you fancy going down the Peter Tobin tonight?"

"No, me and the boys are going down the Fred West, they've just re-paved the beer garden."

Visitors to Edinburgh should soon look out for **The Peter Sutcliffe**, **The Harold Shipman** and **The Bible John.**

Ian Rankin

IAN RANKIN'S NOVELS, AND THEIR CENTRAL character, hard-drinking detective John Rebus, chart the darker, seamier side to Edinburgh life.

Scratch the veneer of respectability in the genteel old city and all kinds of depravity can be found lurking underneath. And it is a city much of whose tourist industry is based around its gruesome, murderous past.

Yet, dark events happen in the present day. Just after New Year 2009, a woman's head was found inside a carrier bag on the Water of Leith walkway.

More specifically, her head was found in an Ikea bag.

How Edinburgh is that?

"Look, Alastair, I don't care what you've got yourself involved with. I don't want the neighbours finding out that we shop at Aldi. If you're thinking of disposing of the torso, there's a Jenners' bag under the kitchen sink."

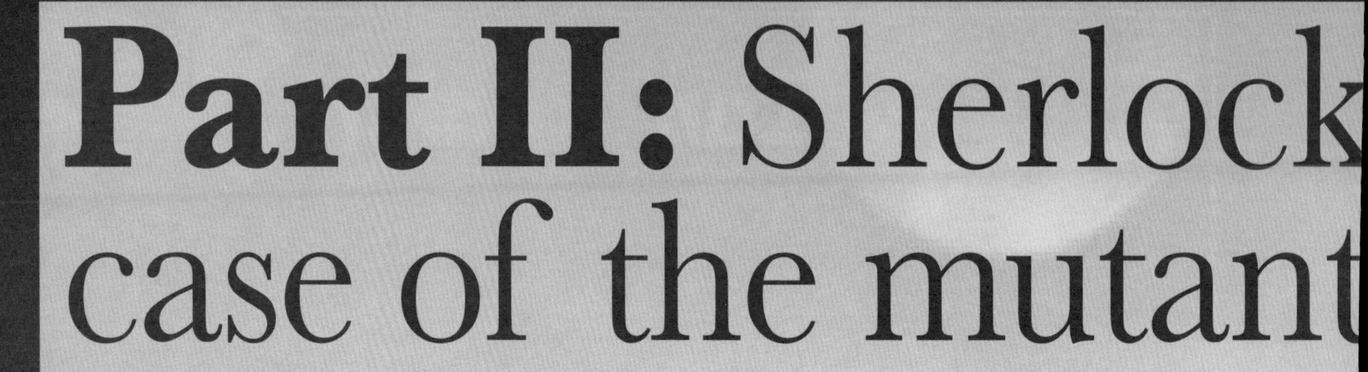

Part II: Sherlock case of the mutant

CONTINUED... (From Page 11)

WATSON AND I WERE ENJOYING A celebratory sherry, and I had just lit a pipe. Content in our success in finding the killer so swiftly and enjoying what remained of a most peaceful Sunday. The calm and quiet was slightly disturbed,

however, by a strange rhythmic banging noise, accompanied by breathless panting, which appeared to emanate from the other side of the wall.

"Whatever can be happening in Miss Stevenson's parlour, Holmes?" queried Watson.

"I don't know, Watson but I would surmise that our hostess is taking her regular weekend's exercise. I did spy a set of ropes hanging from her door as I passed this morning. I am assuming she uses them for skipping."

"Of course, Holmes, I hadn't considered that. Do you know I had the bizarre notion she might be engaged in sexual congress."

"Oh, Watson, don't be so preposterous. Miss Stevenson is both a spinster and a fine upstanding lady."

At this, we could plainly hear our hostess screaming from the adjacent room, "Oh Lord! Oh God! Oh Jesus!"

"And, as you can hear, Watson, a devout Christian to boot."

It was at this moment, that there came a loud knock on th front door.

"Cover up, girls, it's the cops!" came a shout from upstairs And, indeed, it was Inspector McLaverty himself who stood the threshold.

"What is it, McLaverty?" I shouted at him through the ope upstairs window.

"You must come at once, Mr Holmes!" he shouted back. " grave error has been made! We arrested the wrong person! The killer has struck again!"

Watson and I wasted no time in joining him on the street.

"It's one of our own this time, Mr Holmes," he continued. "This is serious, he's throwing down the gauntlet to us now."

WE MADE HASTE TO THE SCENE OF the crime, where a constable guarded the body of his brutally-butchered fello officer, which by now had been covered by a blanket.

Emotion was clearly etched on the ma face and in his voice, as he told me, "He was a right good copper, Sir."

"Can't have been that good, didn't ev recognise the bloody murderer!" retort McLaverty.

"According to witnesses he was attac from behind, Sir. Fellah that did it looked bit like a chimpanzee, they said."

"Doesn't narrow things down much in t part of town," McLaverty replied.

Watson bent over the corpse to examine He appeared puzzled.

"The body is still warm, and yet from this stiff protrusion in the groin area, I would surmise that rigor mortis has already set in

"No, Sir," interrupted the constable, his v trembling with terror, "ye dinnae understa

Holmes and the monkey murderer

hat's not rigor mortis." And he pulled back the lower half of he blanket to let us see the full extent of the heinous crime ommitted. "It's his truncheon!"

Watson struggled to contain his horror at the sight.

"My God, Holmes, we are dealing with the Devil himself ere. Someone who will murder an officer of the law, and hen insert a standard-issue police truncheon in the victim's rethra."

"Quite so, my dear fellow. In all my years of investigating he most brutal of crimes, I have never come across such epravity."

I'VE ONLY WITNESSED ONE CRIME AS DEPRAVED as this, Mr Holmes, twenty-five years ago. I shiver when I think of it now," offered McLaverty. "It happened at the zoo."

"A murder at the zoological gardens?" I queried.

"Not a murder, although some would say it was a far worse ime," explained McLaverty.

"One of the zookeepers was caught having sex with Millie e Monkey."

"Good Lord" muttered Watson. "The likes of him should be rung up!"

"Sentenced to 20 years transportation to the colonies, sir."

"Sending his kind to Australia? With its abundant wildlife? n sure he never came back to Scotland."

"That's where you're wrong, sir. He was converted to hristianity by missionaries, he's now a minister of the Kirk mself. At St Stephen's in Stockbridge."

"It's the poor monkey I feel sorry for," retorted Watson.

"Rumour has it, the poor animal gave birth to a half-man lf-monkey type creature. It was kept in a special secret ge up at the zoo."

lit my pipe and pondered this new information.

"My goodness, McLaverty, it's staring us in the face!" I claimed.

"What is, Mr Holmes?"

"The murderer. Witnesses have described him as a mpanzee, or half-man half-monkey!"

"Yes, Holmes" countered Watson "but technically a mpanzee is an ape."

"But these people aren't experts on primates, Watson. ey're witnesses to a brutal series of murders. And this ernoon, Watson. Remember, at the zoo..."

The empty cage, Holmes! Good gracious, the beast of ich McLaverty speaks..."

Exactly Watson. It has escaped. And is wreaking its enge on humanity!

And I think I can guess where it will strike next. Laverty, how far is it from here to St Stephen's Church?"

Just five minutes around the corner, Mr Holmes."

Then we must make our way there with the ultimate te. A man's life is at risk!"

e set off at the utmost haste towards the church in question, through the gathering gloom and mist of an Edinburgh evening.

On the horizon, as we made our way north towards the river, we could make out a church spire, and could hear an almighty sound of crashing and banging. And a blood-curdling bestial roar that I can imagine had not been heard since the dawn of civilisation itself.

Approaching the church with trepidation, we had no idea of the horror that lurked within.

"Open the door, Cooper, we know you're in there!" shouted McLaverty, as he banged his fist upon the door of the church.

Yet,, as Watson and myself peered into the church from our vantage point above the knave, we saw no human present, merely a monster wreaking havoc and destruction to a house of God.

"We're coming in now, Cooper!" shouted McLaverty as one of his constables broke down the door, at which point a monster, half-man half-monkey rushed out of the front of the building.

"The game's afoot, Watson!" I exclaimed, as we followed the monster though the dingy back-streets of Scotland's capital city, our pursuit hampered by the ever-encroaching fog.

BUT WE COULD FOLLOW THE TRAIL ALL THE way back to the residence of Miss Stevenson. On entering the kitchen area, we were confronted by a sight of the utmost depravity.

Miss Stevenson lay across her own kitchen table in state of undress, a minister of the church on top of her and a bizarre monkey mutant animal attempting to enter the minister from behind.

"Oh, Mr Holmes,"exclaimed Miss Stevenson "you must think I'm a terrible flirt!"

"Miss Stevenson," I warned, "you are in mortal danger!"

"Don't worry, Mr Holmes, I always insist my clients wear protection."

"But, madam, one of these men is a murderer, and is half-monkey," I retorted.

"I just thought he was fae Fife, ken?" was her enigmatic reply.

This tale does not have a happy ending.

The Rev Cooper was struck off for visiting prostitutes, and the monkey-man mutant was hanged for murder.

Yet his remains are still preserved in Edinburgh's Surgeons' Hall.

"A reminder of how close we are to the animal kingdom," suggested Watson.

"Aye," echoed McLaverty.

THE END

11 Irvine Welsh

IRVINE WELSH'S NOVEL TRAINSPOTTING, published in 1993, redefined how the world viewed Scotland. And how we viewed ourselves.

There is a marvellous scene in the movie where Tommy persuades the other guys to take a train up to the Highlands and then makes them climb a mountain, despite their protests.

At the top, admiring the view, he says, "Doesn't that make you proud to be Scottish?" Which elicits a rant from Renton about not being proud at all to be Scottish, because we have nothing to be proud of.

"The English are wankers, effete arseholes. We, on the other hand have been colonised by wankers. We can't even find a decent country to be colonised by. It's a shit state of affairs, Tommy, and no amount of scenery in the world is going to make up for it."

That pretty much sums up how most of us have felt at some time or another.

10 William Wallace

WILLIAM WALLACE WAS BRAVEHEART PERSONIFIED. He led the resistance during the Wars of Scottish Independence and is today remembered as a patriot and national hero.

As leader of Scotland's army he fought two battles against the English, winning one and losing one.

On September 11th 1297, he defeated the English army at the battle of Stirling Bridge and became Guardian of Scotland serving until his defeat at the Battle of Falkirk.

After several years in hiding, Wallace was eventually captured and executed for treason by the English King, Edward Longshanks, In Smithfield in London.

His preserved head was placed on a pike atop London Bridge.

His limbs were displayed, separately, in Stirling, Aberdeen and those other strongholds of Scottish nationalism - Newcastle upon Tyne and Berwick-upon-Tweed.

Even to this day, Wallace attempts to extract retribution from the innocent descendents of his English murderers.

The Wallace Monument is in sight of the M9, just north of Stirling, and is a major cause of traffic accidents.

Sited just to the right of most drivers' peripheral vision, it causes those who are new to the area to momentarily glance away from the road. As a result, there have been many multiple pile-ups down the years on this stretch and many casualties have been English tourists heading north, each one a victim of Wallace's revenge.

Wallace's career stats show a fifty percent record against England, which is on a par with Willie Ormond and Ally MacLeod in battles against the Auld Enemy. However, MacLeod and Ormond both played the English home and away and McLeod even recorded a victory on English turf in 1977.

So, considering that both of Wallace's battles were played at home, his record was not as good as the Scottish media had hoped for. Had he not been executed, the chances are that a tabloid-led campaign would have ended in him having to resign from the job.

Nowadays, the world knows of William Wallace after the film Braveheart - starring and directed by Australian movie star Mel Gibson.

It won an Oscar for best film but, sadly, didn't win an award for best documentary.

Now Mel Gibson has been fiercely criticised for his Scottish accent in the film.

This is unjust.

True, it is not very good but no one in Scotland has any right to criticise a top movie actor who can't do another country's accent.

So we accept that Mel Gibson's Scottish accent is crap.

But not as bad as...

9 Sean Connery

...SEAN CONNERY'S RUSSIAN ACCENT IN THE *Hunt For Red October*.

Or his Irish accent in *The Untouchables*.

Or his Spanish accent in *Highlander*.

This is the worst example because Sean Connery has spent more time in Spain than in Scotland.

Yet, any time he tries to do the Spanish accent it comes out as Scottish.

But we can never hear a bad word against Sean Connery.

The former Mr Universe contestant is now a Scottish icon and one of the most successful Hollywood actors ever.

And his big breakthrough role was playing secret agent, James Bond.

The vast majority of Scots argue that Connery is the best-ever Bond – usually with irony adding the fact that a Scot is the best portrayal of the suave Englishman.

But James Bond had a Scottish father and was educated at Fettes College in Edinburgh – so he is as Scottish as Tony Blair.

After Bond, Sean Connery and his vocal skills continued to make great movies and he never lived in Scotland again.

But he also never lost his accent.

tp://007.da.ru

Tom Weir 8

TOM WEIR LOVED SCOTLAND. A WORKING-class boy from Springburn, he used to think nothing of hiking all the way from North-East Glasgow to the Campsies or Loch Lomond, walking for several miles before he actually started his "walk".

Tom Weir was hugely influential in the rambling movement in Scotland, and he carved out a new career in the 1970s and 80s presenting that marvellous programme on STV – Weir's Way.

A television programme with appallingly bad production values, really tacky editing but what came across loud and clear was Tom Weir's passion for the highlands.

The show has been repeated in subsequent years usually in that post-pub slot where students have come home from a night out and are smoking a joint.

And a new fanbase for Tom Weir has grown.

Tom Weir is a man I have the utmost respect for.

His enthusiasm for the highlands was contagious.

In fact, I'm a such a huge fan, that I felt compelled to create this affectionate homage.

TOM WEIRD: *Hello, well here I am in the picturesque village of Buckie on the North-East coast of Scotland. A gie bracing windy place...*

Over there the raging waters of the North Sea and behind me here the gentler waters of the Moray Firth.

And it's a place steeped in history. Bonnie Prince Charlie spent the night here on his way to the battle of Culloden.

And only two miles down the coast from here was the battle of Ganto, where the redcoat army escaped on their bicycles and were chased by the giant jelly baby... all the way to Berwick-upon-Tweed.

But I'm here today on a blustery windy day where the air is like champagne.

It's a gorgeous place to be and spend a bit of time.

And I'm here to meet Angus McKenzie. Him and his two sons have been fishing out of these waters for over 20 years.

And here he is now. Hello, Angus!

ANGUS: *Hello there, Tam!*

TOM WEIRD: *Hello, Angus!*

TOM WEIRD: *Hello, Angus!*

ANGUS: *Hello there, Tam!*

TOM WEIRD: *Well, Angus as well as being a local fisherman of great repute you are also the custodian of the local history society here.*

ANGUS: *That I am, aye.*

TOM WEIRD: *But your biggest story is that you and your two boys have fished these waters here with probably the biggest fishing fleet on this stretch of coastline. And the boys are they still in the fishing?*

ANGUS: *Och no Tam, they are in Saughton prison noo.*

TOM WEIRD: *Ahh, right...*

ANGUS: *It's for the best, Tam.*

TOM WEIRD: *You had a big fishing fleet and is that the still the case to this day?*

ANGUS: *Well no, Tam, the fishing is no so good, I've had to diversify.*

TOM WEIRD: *Diversify? So what is it you are bringing ashore these days?*

ANGUS: *Well, Tam, smack and Eastern European whores.*

TOM WEIRD: *It's good to see the traditional way of life is still being kept alive.*

ANGUS: *Well you know me, Tam. Too old to change.*

TOM WEIRD: *Thank you very much Angus, it's been good talking to you. Cheerio, Angus!*

ANGUS: *Cheerio now, Tam!*

Robert Louis Stevenson 7

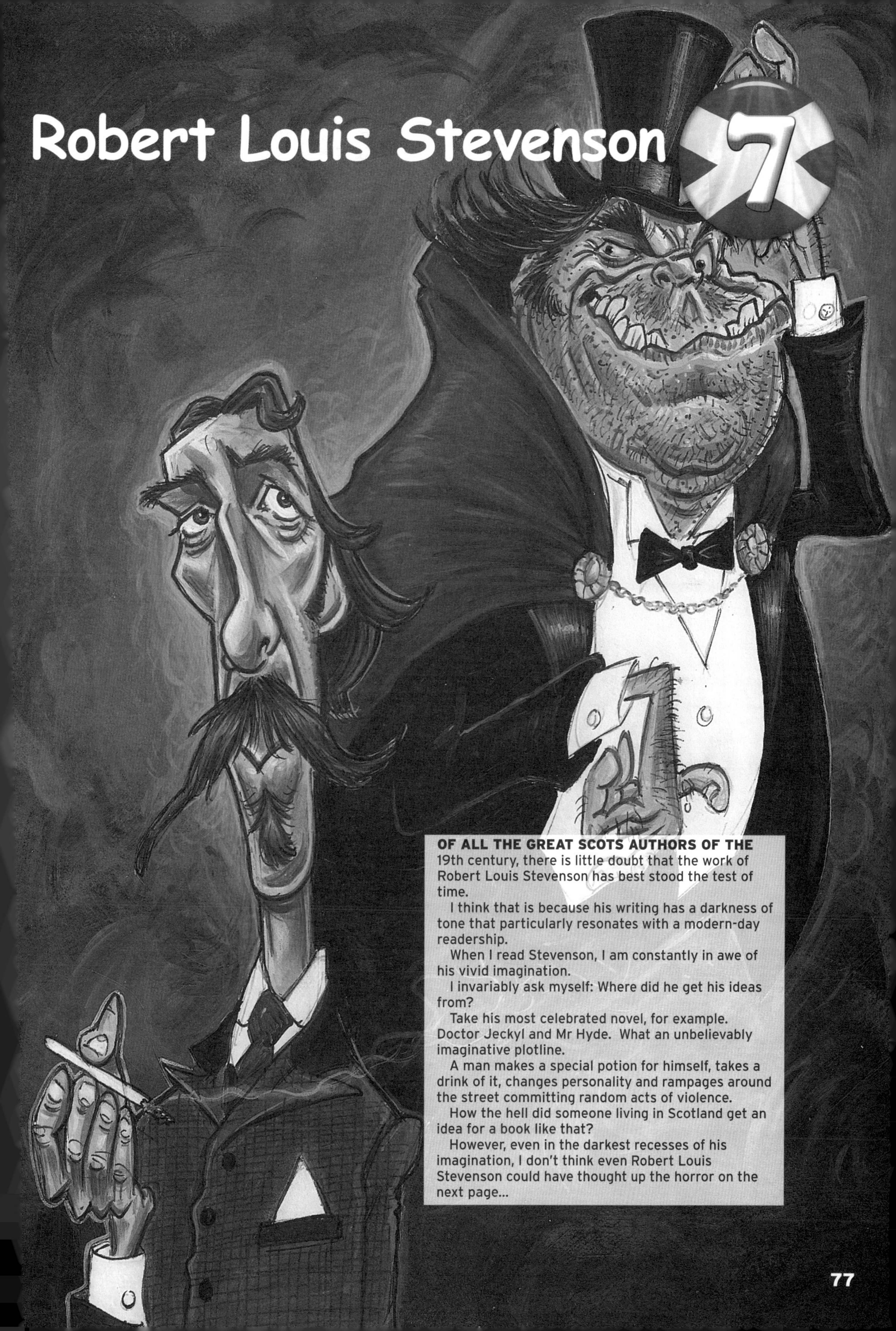

OF ALL THE GREAT SCOTS AUTHORS OF THE 19th century, there is little doubt that the work of Robert Louis Stevenson has best stood the test of time.

I think that is because his writing has a darkness of tone that particularly resonates with a modern-day readership.

When I read Stevenson, I am constantly in awe of his vivid imagination.

I invariably ask myself: Where did he get his ideas from?

Take his most celebrated novel, for example. Doctor Jeckyl and Mr Hyde. What an unbelievably imaginative plotline.

A man makes a special potion for himself, takes a drink of it, changes personality and rampages around the street committing random acts of violence.

How the hell did someone living in Scotland get an idea for a book like that?

However, even in the darkest recesses of his imagination, I don't think even Robert Louis Stevenson could have thought up the horror on the next page...

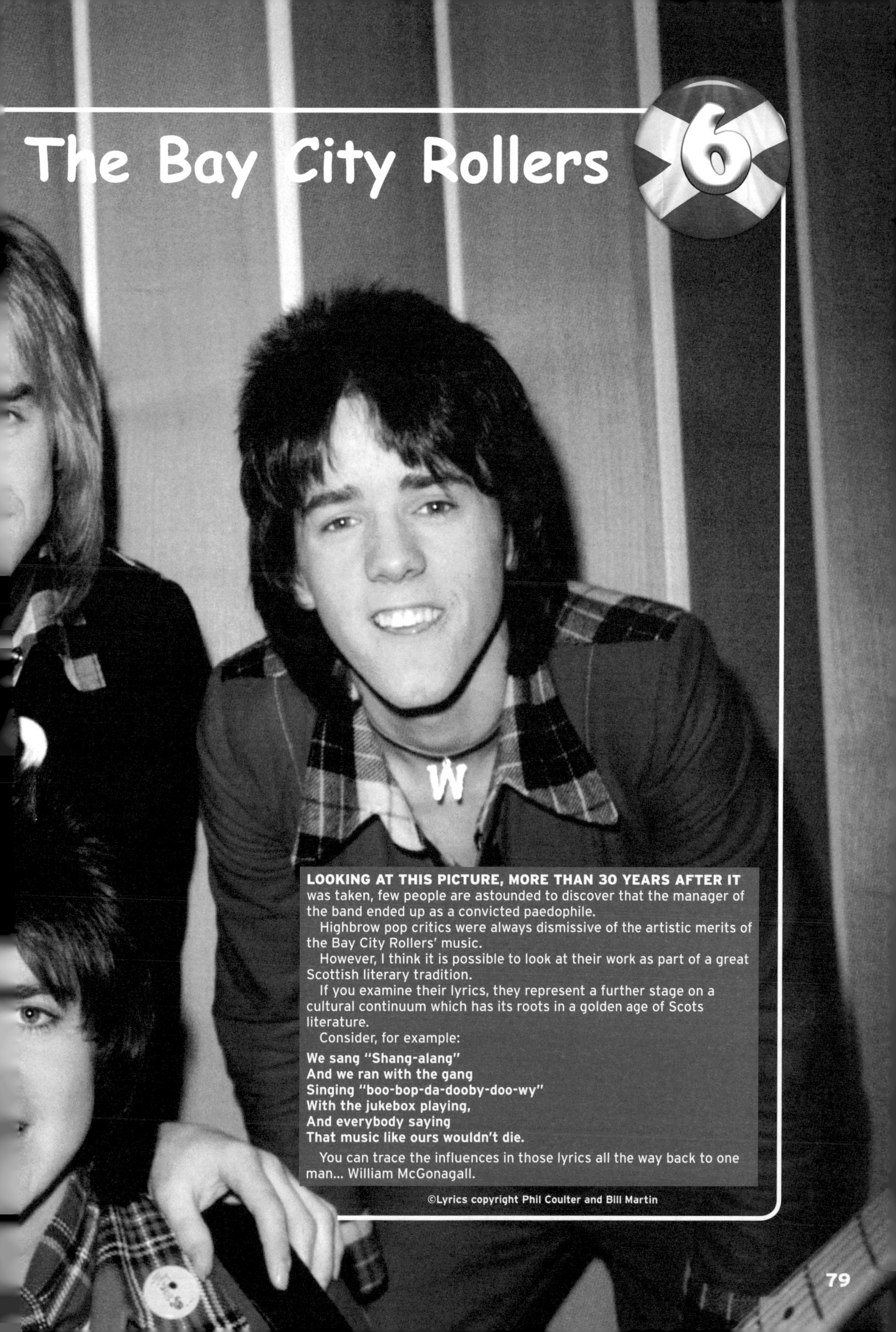

The Bay City Rollers

6

LOOKING AT THIS PICTURE, MORE THAN 30 YEARS AFTER IT was taken, few people are astounded to discover that the manager of the band ended up as a convicted paedophile.

Highbrow pop critics were always dismissive of the artistic merits of the Bay City Rollers' music.

However, I think it is possible to look at their work as part of a great Scottish literary tradition.

If you examine their lyrics, they represent a further stage on a cultural continuum which has its roots in a golden age of Scots literature.

Consider, for example:

We sang "Shang-alang"
And we ran with the gang
Singing "boo-bop-da-dooby-doo-wy"
With the jukebox playing,
And everybody saying
That music like ours wouldn't die.

You can trace the influences in those lyrics all the way back to one man… William McGonagall.

©Lyrics copyright Phil Coulter and Bill Martin

WILLIAM TOPAZ MCGONAGALL WAS A UNIQUE TALENT. Probably borderline mentally ill, definitely seriously deluded but fantastic entertainment nonetheless.

McGonagall not only considered himself to be a great poet, he also styled himself as an 'actor and tragedian'.

He used to perform live readings of his poems in pubs where he would intersperse his poetry with rants about the evils of the demon drink. Unsurprisingly, he was usually bottled off after a few minutes.

Whether his poems were meant to be comic or tragic matters little to a modern-day audience.

Let us just sit back, read and enjoy, his greatest tome:

The Tay Bridge Disaster

Beautiful Railway Bridge of the Silv'ry Tay!
Alas! I am very sorry to say
That ninety lives have been taken away
On the last Sabbath day of 1879,
Which will be remember'd for a very long time.

'Twas about seven o'clock at night,
And the wind it blew with all its might,
And the rain came pouring down,
And the dark clouds seem'd to frown,
And the Demon of the air seem'd to say- "I'll blow down the Bridge of Tay."

When the train left Edinburgh The passengers' hearts were light and felt no sorrow, But Boreas blew a terrific gale, Which made their hearts for to quail, And many of the passengers with fear did say- "I hope God will send us safe across the Bridge of Tay."

But when the train came near to Wormit Bay,
Boreas he did loud and angry bray,
And shook the central girders of the Bridge of Tay
On the last Sabbath day of 1879, Which will be remember'd for a very long time.

So the train sped on with all its might,
And Bonnie Dundee soon hove in sight, And the passengers' hearts felt light,
Thinking they would enjoy themselves on the New Year,
With their friends at home they lov'd most dear,
And wish them all a happy New Year.

So the train mov'd slowly along the Bridge of Tay,
Until it was about midway,
Then the central girders with a crash gave way,
And down went the train and passengers into the Tay.
The Storm Fiend did loudly bray,
Because ninety lives had been taken away,
On the last Sabbath day of 1879,
Which will be remember'd for a very long time.

As soon as the catastrophe came to be known
The alarm from mouth to mouth was blown,
And the cry rang out all o'er the town,
Good Heavens! the Tay Bridge is blown down,
And a passenger train from Edinburgh,
Which fill'd all the peoples hearts with sorrow,
And made them for to turn pale,
Because none of the passengers were sav'd to tell t
tale
How the disaster happen'd on the last Sabbath day o
1879,
Which will be remember'd for a very long time.

It must have been an awful sight,
To witness in the dusky moonlight,
While the Storm Fiend did laugh, and angry did bray,
Along the Railway Bridge of the Silv'ry Tay,
Oh! ill-fated Bridge of the Silv'ry Tay,
I must now conclude my lay
By telling the world fearlessly without the least dismay,
That your central girders would not have given way,
At least many sensible men do say,
Had they been supported on each side with buttresses,
At least many sensible men confesses,
For the stronger we our houses do build,
The less chance we have of being killed.

William McGonagall

5

The value of McGonagall's work today, aside from its car-crash appeal, is that it acts as a window into life in 19th-century Scotland.

Few people learned about the Tay Bridge disaster from history books. Most people know about it solely because of McGonagall's poem.

I have often speculated about what McGonagall would be doing had he been alive today. He would probably be sectioned, auditioning for the X-Factor or taking part in Big Brother. Or all three.

One thing is for certain; he would be writing poetry about current events in the Scotland of his day. With this in mind, I took the liberty a couple of years ago, to write a poem in the style of McGonagall.

It chronicled a momentous event in Scottish history which had recently occurred.

Ladies and gentlemen, I give you...

The Great Spoiled Ballot Paper Fiasco of the Scottish Parliamentary Election of 2007

In 1997, the Scots constitution
Was rewritten by the Act Of Devolution
"There shall be a Scottish Parliament"
The First Minister Donald Dewar said
But alas before it opened he was sadly dead.
Although his statue now stands in Buchanan Street in Glasgow
Often with a traffic cone on his head

When the building opened people came from all around
To see what they were getting for their four hundred million pound
They flocked to Edinburgh to visit Holyrood
But when they saw it many said "I don't think it's that good"

The nation's leaders gathered there to talk
Unless they had gone on holiday with Kirsty Wark
Each member carrying out their parliamentary role
Apart from Tommy Sheridan who according to some salacious stories in the tabloid papers was allegedly down in Manchester getting his hole

In 2007 election day
Was set for Thursday the 3rd of May
But it caused many people much distress and dismay
The spoiled ballot papers numbered 120, 673
The same as the population of Bonnie Dundee
Which the English treated with very much glee

South of the border they did laugh and did gloat
Saying bloody Jocks don't even know how to vote
But it's wrong to blame the entire population
For a highly confusing system of proportional representation

THE PROCLAIMERS ARE AN INSPIRATION TO THE whole of Scotland, and to Scots throughout the world.

The first time I heard them on the radio in the 1980s, it was so exciting to hear rock music being sung in Scottish accents.

Their music defines us as a nation. It celebrates our good points. It never shies away from pointing out our flaws. It is patriotic without being chauvinistic.

A couple of years ago, there was a debate as to what would be the best choice for an official national anthem for Scotland.

The choices were fairly predictable:

Flower of Scotland, a song which harks back to a time of war against England.

Scots Wh' Ha'e, an inspiring song but one which too harks back to a time of war against England.

I don't think a modern nation should have that kind of sentiment in its national anthem.

If that's the message you want to convey, you may as well go the whole way and make Scotland's national anthem *If You Hate the Fucking English Clap Your Hands.*

The Proclaimers wrote a song, *Scotland's Story,* which I believe would make an ideal national anthem.

It celebrates the multicultural nature of modern Scotland,

Michael McGrory from west Donegal
You came to Glasgow with nothing at all
You fought the landlord then the Afrika korps
When you came to Glasgow with nothing at all

Abraham Caplan from Vilnius you came
You were heading for New York but Leith's where you've stayed
You built a great business which benefits all
Since you came to this land with nothing at all

In Scotland's Story I read that they came

The Proclaimers 4

he Gael and the Pict, the Angle and Dane
ut so did the Irishman, Jew and Ukraine
hey're all Scotland's Story and they're all worth the same

oseph D'Angelo dreams of the days
'hen Italian kids in the Grassmarket played
'e burned out his shop when the boys went to war
ut auld Joe's a big man and he forgave all

Scotland's Story I'm told that they came
he Gael and the Pict, the Angle and Dane
ut where's all the Chinese and Indian names?
hey're in my land's story and they're all worth the same

hristina McKay, I learned of your name
ow you travelled south from Delny one day
u raised a whole family in one room they say
d the X on the line stands in place of your name

So in the old story I'll bet that I came
From Gael and Pict and Angle and Dane
And a poor migrant girl who could not write her name
It's a common old story but it's mine just the same

All through the story the immigrants came
The Gael and the Pict, the Angle and Dane
From Pakistan, England and from the Ukraine
We're all Scotland's story and we're all worth the same
Your Scotland's Story is worth just the same

©Copyright Charlie Reid/Craig Reid/Chrysalis Records

I think that would make a really fitting national anthem for Scotland. Perhaps with this additional verse for a bit of light relief:

Adrian Buckland from Buckinghamshire
Bought a hotel on the Mull of Kintyre
You fought off the midges and the Settler Watch
When they put burning dog-shite through your letter-box

ACCORDING TO HISTORY, ROBERT THE BRUCE WAS one of our greatest ever kings.

But his right to the throne of Scotland was tenuous, to say the least.

Robert the Bruce claimed the Scottish throne as a fourth great-grandson of David I, which must have made him something like forty-fifth in the line of succession (or slightly further down the pecking order than an illegitimate son of James Hewitt) and he would appear to have hung about in some fairly dubious company.

For a start, he managed to persuade his followers to fight the English at Bannockburn after receiving advice from a spider in a cave.

Which suggests they must have been very loyal, very stupid or shit-scared of the guy.

"Listen, Big Rab says we've to fight the English coz some spider telt him. He's obviously aff his fucking chump but you know how radge he gets when he's been on the Buckie!"

Bruce, furthermore, only became King of Scotland, after he had murdered his rival John Comyn, stabbing him in a fight in a churchyard in Dumfries.

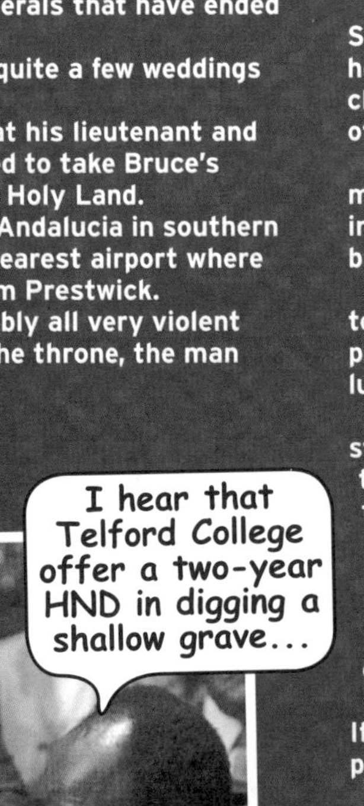

Thankfully, we now have more sophisticated ways of choosing our leaders.

Let's face it, if stabbing people were the only skill required of a king, over 50% of the population of Paisley would be laying claim to the Throne of Scotland.

Bruce's body is buried in Dunfermline Abbey, while his heart is buried in Melrose.

Which suggests that his wake ended up being one enormous rammy, with mourners buggering off with body parts to all four corners of Scotland. But we've all been to funerals that have ended up a bit like that.

Come to think of it, I've been to quite a few weddings that ended up a bit like that.

Actually, what happened was that his lieutenant and 'friend', Sir James Douglas, decided to take Bruce's embalmed heart on crusade to the Holy Land.

But they only reached as far as Andalucia in southern Spain. Presumably that was the nearest airport where they could get a Ryanair flight from Prestwick.

While our early kings were probably all very violent men with a questionable right to the throne, the man who claimed to be the Last King of Scotland, was one of the most fearsome despots of the twentieth century. Of course, we all know that this was Ugandan tyrant IDI AMIN.

A man whose crime against his own citizens included having one of his archbishops executed and then eating his liver. Puts Bruce's achievements in the shade somewhat.

Strangely, Scotland as a nation has a number of connections to African dictators.

For example in the 1980s, Robert Mugabe was awarded an honorary degree by the University of Edinburgh. However, in 2007 they withdrew the award as a protest against his appalling record on human rights.

Which will have stopped his nonsense overnight.

Bound up in the mythology and legend of the Scottish throne, Scots sat on the stone to be crowned.

Of course, Amin's claim to be King of Scotland was utterly false. Because, of course, he had never sat on the Stone of Destiny

Housed in Scone Palace, the Stone of Destiny was looted by Edward I in 1296. It is thought this was a fake, as the original had been hidden and replaced by a random lump of rock.

The random lump of rock that the English thought to be the Stone of Destiny remained in Westminster Abbey until Chirstmas Day 1950.

It was then stolen in the dead of night by a group of young SNP activists.

When tracked down by the police, they later returned it but it is thought they may have hidden it and replaced it with another fake. So what we have is a copy of a copy.

The fake, fake Stone of Destiny was finally returned to Scotland in 1992 by Tory Prime Minister John Major, as he rather short-sightedly thought this would stop the clamour for devolution and/or compensate for the tyrann of the Thatcher years. Of course it did neither.

Compared to most of the other Prime Ministers of modern times, John Major was never famed for his intellect, having failed in his attempt to become a London bus conductor.

However, even he should have been bright enough to work out that if a nation is clamouring for its own parliament that the people are not going to settle for a lump of granite as a substitute.

The clamour for the return of the Stone always did strike me as being a supreme irrelevance. Its only use is to crown the monarch of Scotland who nine times out of ten hasn't been Scottish in the first place.

Indeed the two current contenders for the title are th Queen (who grew up in England but is ethnically Germa or some bloke in Belgium who claims to be descended from Charles Edward Stuart but who can't speak a wor of either English or Gaelic and is clearly disturbed.

And we bother about the ownership of a lump of rock. If the Stone of Destiny has any significance, it lies in its place in Scottish myth and folklore.

According to ancient legend, the Stone of Destiny was originally Jacob's pillow and was brought over to Scotlar from the Holy Land. In other words, we nicked it in the first place. In that case, the only sensible course of acti is to send it back to the Palestinians.

At least they'll get some use out of it, by chucking it a Israeli tanks.

Bad news, Sir, Edinburgh University have taken away your degree!
I hear that Telford College offer a two-year HND in digging a shallow grave...
This is awful, I can no longer carry out genocide on my own people! I am not qualified!

Robert the Bruce 3

SCRIPT: PS / ART: AC

Oor Wullie 2

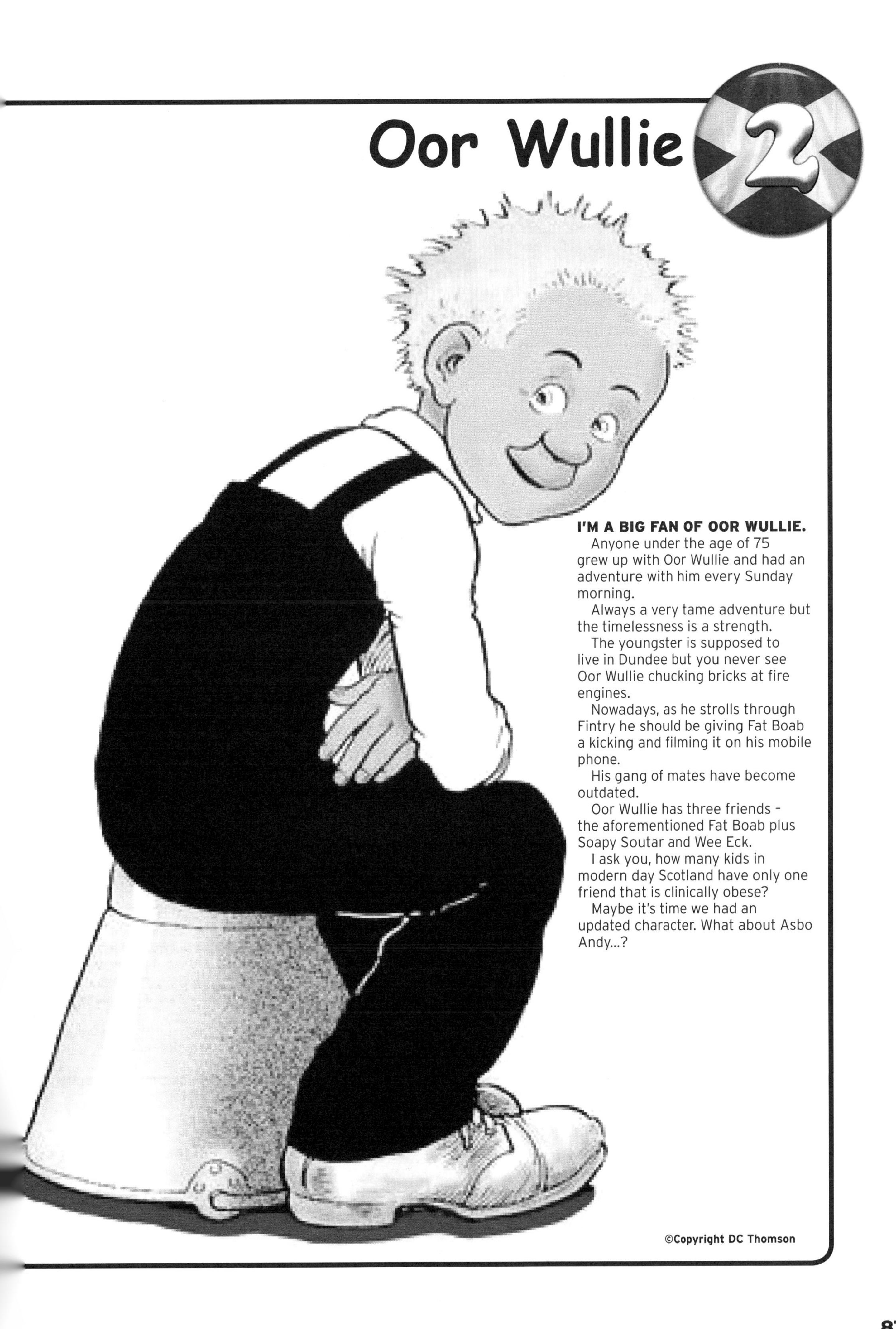

I'M A BIG FAN OF OOR WULLIE.

Anyone under the age of 75 grew up with Oor Wullie and had an adventure with him every Sunday morning.

Always a very tame adventure but the timelessness is a strength.

The youngster is supposed to live in Dundee but you never see Oor Wullie chucking bricks at fire engines.

Nowadays, as he strolls through Fintry he should be giving Fat Boab a kicking and filming it on his mobile phone.

His gang of mates have become outdated.

Oor Wullie has three friends – the aforementioned Fat Boab plus Soapy Soutar and Wee Eck.

I ask you, how many kids in modern day Scotland have only one friend that is clinically obese?

Maybe it's time we had an updated character. What about Asbo Andy...?

©Copyright DC Thomson

Bubbling under: Part 2

TENSE MOMENTS, AS WE AWAIT THE IDENTITY of our number One Sweaty. So let's pause and look at some more names bubbling under our list...

COLIN MONTGOMERIE

DIDN'T MAKE THE CUT. BUT THEN, THAT'S becoming an all-too-frequent occurrence these days.

On the subject of Monty, another famous Scot to miss out on selection is someone to whom he has been frequently compared... MRS DOUBTFIRE

SAM TORRANCE

ANOTHER GOLFING SCOT WORTHY OF SPECIAL mention is SAM TORRANCE, if not for his prowess on the links, then for his attitude and commitment off course.

After captaining Europe to victory in the 2002 Ryder Cup, Sam by his own admission celebrated by going on a "three-day bender".

It's reassuring to see the Corinthian spirit (or should that be spirits?) still living on in the 21st Century.

In a nation with such a fondness for booze, and which takes justifiable pride in the range and quality of its whiskies, it seems strange that not one distiller rates a mention.

But let's face it, if we hadn't invented whisky, we'd just have found something else to get shit-faced on. In fact it's amazing we ever sobered-up enough to discover the art of distilling (given that's it's a secondary process).

Of course we didn't only invent whisky. We invented the raincoat, tarmacadam and the pneumatic tyre.

William Dunlop's original invention was seen as merely a contribution towards comfort and safety on the road.

Little did he know how much it would influence our wider culture and enhance the lives of many women, among them

JORDAN & PAMELA ANDERSON

I AM AWARE THERE ARE MORE HISTORICAL figures who have had a major impact on the nation's development.

People such as Emperor Hadrian, not Scottish but a man who profoundly changed our relationship with England.

By building a fucking big wall between us.

Another ancient Roman, Pontius Pilate, was actually Scottish.

He was born in Perthshire. The Roman army got as far north as the Antonine Wall in central Scotland, where Pilate was recruited into one of their legions. He made his way up the career structure and ended up the governor of Palestine during the crucifixion.

Now I think Pilate was wrongly blamed for the crucifixion. It wasn't his fault at all – he was just hosting the whole event.

It was the crowd that chose who was going to the gallows, wasn't it?

To blame Pilate for the crucifixion is like blaming Ant and Dec for the result of *Britain's Go Talent*.

We've got a quite a lot to thank the guy for. Anyone who looks forward to their four-day break over Easter should remember that they wouldn't have got that without Pontius Pilate.

MICHAEL JACKSON

NO-ONE WOULD CLAIM THAT MICHAEL JACKSO had any connection with Scotland.

However, it was Scots author J.M.Barrie who was the inspiration behind his life's work.

It was Barrie, after all, who wrote Peter Pan, an created Neverland.

Without his influence, Wacko Jacko's life would have been very mundane indeed.

Because Michael Jackson was such a weirdo when alive, people can make ridiculous claims about him, and they will be credible.

The most bizarre statement sounds believable if you precede it with three words. Those three words are "Apparently Michael Jackson".

"Apparently Michael Jackson had a pet unicorr Apparently Michael Jackson had a bath every morning in llama's milk.

Apparently Michael Jackson's nose was originally Elizabeth Taylor's clitoris"

JIMMY SHAND

A TRULY LEGENDARY SCOTTISH MUSICIAN Jimmy Shand sadly does not make it into our To 50.

Still revered throughout Scotland as the King of the Accordian, it is very difficult to find anyon in Scotland with a bad word to say about Jimmy Shand. It was impossible to get angry about Jimmy Shand. Unless of course you lived next door to him!

"Hey, you! Ya baldy bastard! Can you pack in playing your fucking squeezebox? It's half past two in the bloody morning!"

A number of great Scots inventors and innovators fail to make our chart.

SIR JAMES SIMPSON

MEN SUCH AS SIR JAMES SIMPSON WHO pioneered the use of chloroform, which in its da was a revolutionary drug.

This was, after all, long before Scottish men

were able to buy rohypnol.

The entire industrial revolution can be seen as the legacy of JAMES WATT, who invented the first working steam engine.

Without Watt's innovation, large-scale industrialisation and heavy engineering would have been impossible.

Many will be aware that it was a Scot KIRKPATRICK MACMILLAN who invented the bicycle.

Yet some Scots innovators remain virtually unknown.

It will come as a shock to most customers of the Ann Summers, for example, to discover that suspenders were actually invented by an ageing crofter in Orkney.

However, local recordings from the 1880s tell how local eccentric Davie Taylor invented 'a bib and brace sort of clasp for hooking his breeks up'.

DAVID STEEL

THE LIBERAL MP FOR ROXBURGH, SELKIRK and Peebles paved the way for legalised abortion.

The 1967 Abortion Act, which he introduced to Parliament, brought an end to back-street terminations.

It was, however met by a great deal of opposition in Scotland. From the Catholic Church, from the Free Presbyterians.

And from the owners of a coathanger factory in Galashiels.

Many Scots are more revered abroad than they are at home.

Olympic sprinter ERIC LIDDELL is better known in China as a Christian missionary.

Liddell is, of course, immortalised in the 1980s movie *Chariots of Fire*.

At the 1924 Olympics, in Paris, Liddell won the gold medal in the 400 metres, which he ran in a world record time of 47.6 seconds.

This stood as a Scottish record until the 1990s, when another Scotsman, from Drumchapel, ran a mile in 47.6 seconds, in an attempt to escape from the Child Support Agency.

JOHN PAUL JONES

SCOTSMAN JOHN PAUL JONES IS ONE OF the great heroes of the American Revolution, and was the founder of the US Navy.

Born in Kirkcudbright, on the northern side of the Solway Firth, one of the first orders he issued was for the American fleet to fire on the English port of Whitehaven, on the southern side of the Solway.

Which is going a hell of a long way to settle a local grudge.

Other Scots who helped shape the New World, include JOHN BUCHAN, who as well as being a

renowned author was also Governor-General of Canada. SIR JOHN ALEXANDER MACDONALD, Canada's first Prime Minister, and MAJOR GENERAL LACHLAN MACQUARRIE, known as "The Father of Australia" were also Scots.

It seems particularly apt that a nation of aggressively Anglophobic binge-drinkers should consider a Scotsman to be their father!

And though one Scot has boldly gone into space, he's not found space in our Top 50.

NEIL ARMSTRONG

THE FIRST MAN TO SET FOOT ON THE MOON, Neil Armstrong had strong family links to the town of Langholm, in the Borders.

After landing on the moon, Armstrong was awarded the Freedom of the Burgh of Langholm. Armstrong himself claimed that visiting the town in his youth had been ideal preparation for the lunar mission.

Because, when he landed on the moon, he found it actually had more atmosphere than Langholm.

SCOTT OF THE ANTARCTIC

CAPT ROBERT HENRY FALCON SCOTT CHOSE to die at the South Pole rather than live in Dundee. And frankly, who can blame him ?

There was no room in the book for Scott of the Antarctic but then that is the story of his life - other people getting there before him.

All of this proves my original premise that Scotland has punched above its weight in so many fields.

And the fact so many explorers have come from Scotland also bears out the general assumption that life in Scotland can be routinely bleak.

After all, how shit must life have been in this country in the Victorian era for people to choose the searing heat of the African sun or the all-numbing cold of the Polar ice-cap over life in Presbyterian Scotland of the time?

LORD KELVIN

A SCOTTISH SCIENTIST GREATLY REVERED in the USA is Lord Kelvin.

His name is still used by a brand of refrigerator.

Kelvin evolved his very own temperature scale, which redefined "Absolute Zero" at minus 273 degrees centigrade.

It really should come as no surprise that a Scot should want to come up with a scientific definition of "Absolutely Fucking Baltic"

But overcoming the dreichness of Scottish life has been a challenge for all of us.

None more so than our Number One...

RABBIE BURNS IS THE EMBODIMENT OF MUCH OF what is good about Scotland and a lot about what is not so good about Scotland.

He is a Scottish everyman. He has transcended time and geographical boundaries.

His work has been covered by modern day artists such as Lou Reed and Patti Smith.

And still, years after his birth, he was single-handedly leading Scotland out of recession.

Homecoming Scotland 2009 was an events programme hoping to boost Scotland's tourist industry.

Its headline promotion was that the entire festival had been created to celebrate Burns' 250th anniversary.

That's an amazing responsibility for someone who has been dead since 1796. But there is no doubt of Burns' influence upon Scotland.

Burns was a very inspiring poet – he wrote incredibly moving poetry and romantic verse. And yet he was a drunk and a womaniser.

Burns was very much the Frank McAvennie of the written word. That's something of an oxymoron – Frank McAvennie and the written word.

A guy in Hawick was thrown out of his local Burns Supper for getting drunk and touching up a woman. He was basically thrown out of his local Burns society for behaving like Robert Burns.

The poet's image graces book covers, shortbread tins, plates, ties, and tea-towels and Burns continues to serve as an icon for generations of Scots.

It could be argued his death made him even more Scottish in the eyes of the nation.

He died, age 37, from rheumatic fever which he contracted after falling asleep at the roadside in the pouring rain – after a particularly vigorous drinking session.

And he is a rightful icon for Scots and Scotland as he himself was a complex and contradictory character.

My Love Is Like A Red, Red Rose is regarded as one of the most touching love poems ever written and yet he had 12 children from four different women.

The last of Burns' children was actually born during his funeral service.

He was anti-government and yet worked for a time as a tax collector. He was at times supportive of the notion of the United Kingdom and then later in life a passionate Scottish nationalist.

Anyone who has ever been to Dumfries will not find Burns's behaviour unusual.

Dumfriesians have a unique world view. I was once on stage when a member of the audience took off his false leg, stuck it on his head and exclaimed; "Look at me! I'm the Isle of Man!"

What I find amazing about Burns is not that his works have stood the test of time but that the establishment have embraced him. Even though he was an anti-establishment figure at the time.

If you go to one of those posh exclusive gentlemen's clubs, in say the New Town of Edinburgh, they will have a Burns Supper on the 25th of January.

It will be a very formal affair.

The well-heeled, well-fed, well-dressed members of the ruling classes come together and have a Burns supper.

Imagine the black-tied toff exclaiming:

"Your grace, your lordships, honoured guests, ladies and gentlemen, I would like to thank Farquar McKenzie for his highly entertaining address to the haggis.

In the words of the great bard himself: *'What though on hamely fare we dine, wear hodding grey, an a' that? Gie fools their skills, and knaves their wine - A man's a man for a' that'.*

Now please be upstanding and raise your glasses..."

Burns would have hated that.

He was a political radical who had no time for the ruling classes.

And the ruling classes abhorred Robert Burns during his life.

Not just because he was a political radical but because a number of his words were absolutely X-rated filthy.

They have become sanitised by the passage of time.

The Victorians removed all the filth.

Some of his original poems – especially in the Merry Muses of Caledonia – are a stream of obscenity.

Burns work in the 1700s was every bit as shocking as Trainspotting was in the 1990s.

It's not a great leap of imagination to think that 200 years from now the well-heeled, well-fed, well-dressed members of the ruling classes coming together and holding an Irvine Welsh supper.

Imagine the black-tied toff exclaiming:

"Your grace, your lordships, honoured guests, ladies and gentlemen, I would like to thank Farquar McKenzie for his highly entertaining address to the deep fried Mars Bar.

In the words of the great bard himself:

Choose life.
Choose a job.
Choose a career.
Choose a family.
Choose a fucking big television.
But why would I want to do a thing like that?
I chose not to choose life.
I chose heroin.

Now please be upstanding and find a vein as we jack up in the immortal memory of the Bard, Irvine Welsh."

But while Burns' work may be relevant to the 21st century, I believe we should have a Burns verse for the times in which we live...

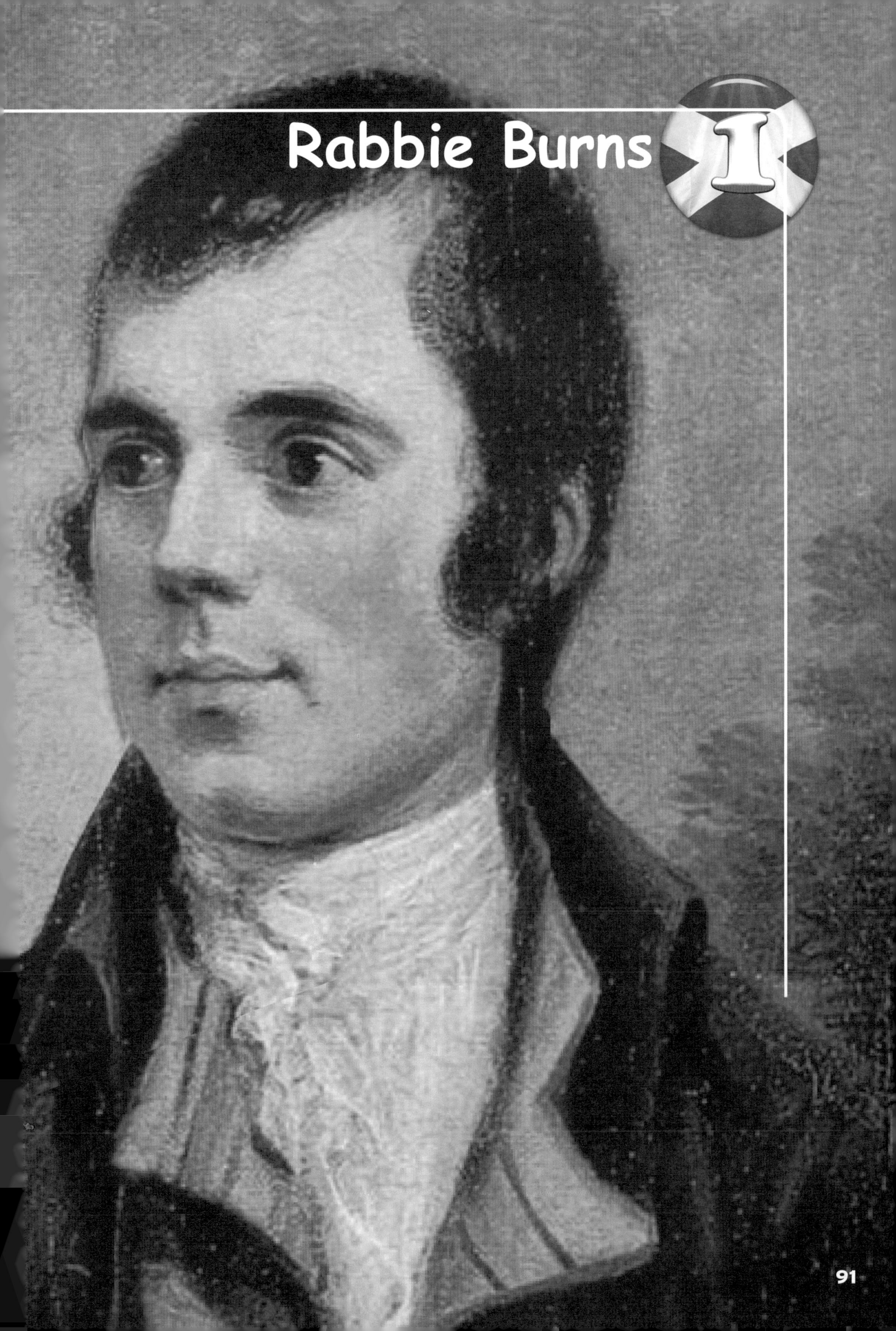
Rabbie Burns

I have tried, where possible, to keep as close as I can to the Bard's original sentiment.

(The Address to the Haggis is really all about trying to get your end away!)

Address To the Deep-Fried Mars Bar

Fair fa' your honest dark brown wrapper
Sweet choclate and gooey matter
Wurk, rest and play ye can mak' 'ur
Or so you've cried
But when you're dunked aboot in batter
And then deep-fried!

Who'd want a fancy French ragout
Or vegans wi' their bland tofu
After sixteen bottles of WKD Blue
There's just one answer
To them that wants a drunken spew
Ya braw wee dancer!

Into the chippy they stagger and fall
Friday night pissed up the wall
Still hoping they might get their hole.
What fuels their ardour?
Tae hell wi' the cholesterol
Gi'e hier a Mars Bar!

Many readers will doubtless also be familiar with "The Selkirk Grace" which is traditionally said at the commencement of a Burns supper.

Some ha'e meat and cannae eat, and some can eat but want it
But we ha'e meat and we can eat.
And so the Lord be thankit.

More appropriate for the 21st Century would be:

The Fred Goodwin Grace

Some ha'e meat and cannae eat
And some can eat that want it
But I ha'e meat and I can eat
So fuck 'em!

Index

Index (continued)